Praise for *The Hope Factor*

"In *The Hope Factor*, Sue Mocker gives a refreshing and unique perspective on how to model and share hope in your life, in your business, and in your relationships. *The Hope Factor* is one woman's courageous journey to heal and find greater meaning through trusting in a personal relationship with Jesus Christ while overcoming horrific adversity. Everyone could benefit from a diet of Hope Pie!"

— **Robin B. O'Grady, Author of**
The Optimist's Edge: Moving Beyond
Negativity to Create Your Amazing Life

"I love the idea of looking for Hope in places I did not think to look and realizing that Hope is everywhere. Each new day gives us opportunities to see the Hope around us."

— **Dr. Leslie Bedell, Chiropractor, Nutritionist, and Cranial**
Sacral Therapist, Agape Chiropractic Healing Center

"Whether you have faith in God or are still searching for what you believe, this book will bring you into a deeper understanding of what you believe on your spiritual journey. This book is truly a gift to humankind and will certainly be the lighthouse of hope during the most challenging times of your life."

— **Patrick Snow, International Best-Selling Author of**
Creating Your Own Destiny **and** *The Affluent Entrepreneur*

"This book will challenge readers to dig deep within themselves to answer some tough questions. This is the beginning of finding Hope."

— **Rodger McCollum, CEO, Superintendent of King County Public Hospital District #4**

"Offering insight, stories, and heartfelt emotions, Sue Mocker's *The Hope Factor* is a powerful book. Sue reminds us of our right to live a joyful life regardless of our past. As she delves into *her* life, she takes you on a journey to explore your own, warts and all. The resulting outcome—five big slices of Hope Pie."

— **Jacqueline Fairbrass, Holistic Health & Wellness Expert at Feeling Absolutely Fabulous**

"Sue, you give voice to the voiceless. Thank you for having the courage to speak out and be heard. Thank you for showing us that adversity sets the stage for victory. Thank you for giving clarity to my thoughts and putting them into words."

— **Al Foxx, Author of** *Achieving No Limits: Embracing Change*

"The Bible says: Faith is the substance of things hoped for. I believe Hope is what gives faith its purpose and direction. Sue Mocker's book *The Hope Factor* gives you the tools and encouragement to transform your life and find your direction. This is a must-read for anyone needing a compass, and well, HOPE."

— **Dr. Eric J. Scroggins, Author of** *Vision Blockers: How to Shatter Barriers to Achieve Your Destiny*

"Sue's strength and courage to pen these words of truth will bring hope, healing, and forgiveness."

— **Sue Stults, Inspirational Speaker and CEO of Compelled by Compassion**

"Hope is a big topic. Sue Mocker does a great job, bringing a fresh perspective to what hope is, how one can find it, and how to pass it on."

— **Jewels Muller, MA, Chief Chick of Chicks Connect and Author of *The Easy Way to Organize* and *The ABCs of Parenting***

"Sue Mocker provides practical steps for finding hope in a hopeless world. If you want to learn more about hope, start here!"

— **Tim Howey, Senior Pastor of Grace Church**

"In order to give Hope, you have to have it. Sue has it and she is inspiring others to give it away. I encourage all of you to read this book—who does not want more HOPE?"

— **Nina Baldwin, Author of *Helping Women Succeed in Business***

"Hope Pie. Five slices to Hope. Brilliant!"

— **Carol Paul, Author of *Team Clean: The Ultimate Family Clean-Up-The-House Formula***

A LEADERSHIP ROADMAP TO HEALING AND SELF-DISCOVERY

The Hope Factor

Discovering the Light through Your Pain

Sue Mocker

The Hope Factor:
Discovering the Light through Your Pain
Copyright 2014 by Sue Mocker
All rights reserved

Address inquiries to:
Sue Mocker
P.O. Box 165
North Bend, WA 98045
425-246-9355
sue@hopeallowed.com
www.HopeAllowed.com

Names and details of incidents in this book have been changed, except those for which permission has been granted. Any similarity between the names and stories, where changes have been made, in this book to individuals known to readers is purely coincidental.

Paperback Cover ISBN: 978-1-938686-72-6
Hard Cover ISBN: 978-1-938686-73-3
eBook ISBN: 978-1-938686-74-0
Library of Congress Control Number: 2014909518

Editor: Tyler Tichelaar
Cover/Jacket design and cover photo: Lindsey Larson
Interior design and layout: Fusion Creative Works

Every attempt has been made to source properly all quotes.
All Scripture references are from the King James Version (KJV) of the Bible.

Printed in the United States of America
For additional copies visit:
www.TheHopeFactor.com

Published by Aviva Publishing
Lake Placid, NY
518-523-1320
www.avivapubs.com

DEDICATION

To Jesus, my Savior, and all of the people in my life who boldly invited me to church, talked to me about my faith, discipled me, and provided me with the tools of faith. I love you all.

To the love of my life, Frank: my husband, friend, and confidant. Thank you for encouraging me, supporting me, and loving me. I love that God gave us to each other.

To my daughters, you are so precious and have challenged me to become a better mom and a better person. I am forever grateful God has indescribably blessed me.

To Mom and Dad, thank you for encouraging me to go places I didn't think I could go, showing me grace while I learn and grow from my mistakes, and loving me no matter what. I am blessed to have you in my life.

To the reader, it is an honor and privilege to come alongside you on this journey of discovering the light through your pain. You are very brave.

ACKNOWLEDGMENTS

"The Lord gave the word: great was the company of those that published it."

— **Psalm 68:11**

When I decided to write a book, I had no idea what I was getting myself into. It soon became very clear to me that this undertaking was not going to be accomplished without a lot of help.

Patrick Snow, my publishing coach, you have guided me through the process of writing this book. Wow, what a ride! I did not realize when I hired you, Patrick, that I was entering into a whole family of other like-minded authors who would encourage me every step of the way. Thank you.

Robin O'Grady, I remember the day we met! Getting to know you through the writing process has been a joy beyond imagination. I have gained a new sister in my life. Thank you.

Lindsey Larson, working with you on my cover design and other branding designs is a gift I will treasure always. Thank you.

To all of those along the way who helped guide me through many challenging times, I thank you.

CONTENTS

FOREWORD

by Patrick Snow

When I was a young boy at thirteen years old, I learned firsthand the power behind the word "Hope." I received a clear understanding of the true meaning of hope and how to apply it, especially during the dark and difficult times in my life. Hope has served me well over the years and has helped me to pursue my dreams and live with passion.

It was May 29, 1982 when my life forever changed, the evening my loving mother, Lois Snow, used hope to get our family through a major crisis. I was the fourth of five children, and I grew up with loving parents in a middle-class Michigan family in your basic 1980s neighborhood. That night, a drunk driver crashed his red truck into the side of our house at an estimated speed of forty miles per hour. His truck struck our gas meter dead-on center and broke the gas line.

As a result, our family home with all of us inside, either sleeping or soon to go to bed, exploded into a gigantic ball of flames. Fortunately, my entire family managed to get out of the house in time, and then we stood and watched the fire consume our home. One entire side of our family home burned for ninety minutes before courageous firefighters managed to wedge an axe into the broken gas line and eventually put out the fire. Once the gas line was blocked with the axe, the remainder of the fire was thankfully soon put out as well.

There my entire family stood, speechless in our side yard, as we smelled the odor of smoke and burnt debris. My mother was in her nightgown, and my father was standing in his boxers as both were awakened as a result of the explosion below their bedroom window. My siblings and my cousin and I were just staring at our house, which was half-burned, now had a basement full of water, and smoke damage throughout. Everything that we owned was ruined.

In that moment, my life completely changed forever as I watched my mother huddle our entire family together. With conviction and hope in her voice, she hugged us all and shouted out, "Everything will be okay. You have nothing to worry about; no one has died and we are all safely here together!" In that moment, I truly witnessed hope in action, and I knew that our family would rebound from this adversity. We did, and we are all stronger as a result.

I believe that hope is the number one required ingredient in the recipe to develop a positive and optimistic outlook on life. I also think hope is one of the most powerful words in the English language. People infused with hope can lead others to achieve world peace, mend relationships, heal hearts, and even allow families to stick together and rebuild a home after a devastating house fire. *Hope* is the key for transforming your pain to perseverance.

In this powerful book by Sue Mocker, you will learn how to harness the power of hope and apply it to your life to overcome difficult experiences. A loving wife and mother, passionate and inspiring professional speaker, sought after hope consultant, and successful transformation and change expert, Sue has spent many years following her own advice to achieve personal transformation and success in all areas of her life. She has a heart of gold and is a brilliant problem-solver, among her many other amazing attributes.

In *The Hope Factor*, Sue provides you with a step-by-step system to help you achieve a better life, believe in your potential, and to accept and receive the gifts that God has waiting specifically for you. You will realize your potential and embrace your new life. As your mind, heart, and soul evolve to a new way of thinking, you will learn what is possible for you and hope will become the foundation of your positive outlook and your new life philosophy.

Furthermore, you will learn how to increase the level of your resiliency and apply hope to both your personal and business communications. You will learn to take a leadership role in your life and transform your obstacles into new and exciting opportunities. This book will provide you with many of the answers that you have spent years of your life seeking. Most importantly, this book will teach you how to view your adversity as opportunity, believe in yourself, and stretch your mind to what is possible for you.

So get ready for an exciting journey. Get ready to learn that your present situation is not your final destination. Both Sue and I are convinced that your best days are yet to come. This book will help guide you to your destiny. As you are about to learn, hope not only can transform your life and the lives of those you love, but it can also serve as a mantra and inspiration for world peace as evidenced by Nelson Mandela's final words to his family prior to being taken away to serve twenty-seven years in a South African prison for non-violent protests. He said to his wife and children, *"Be strong and be hopeful."* Sue and I encourage you to do the same.

Enjoy.

Patrick Snow

Patrick Snow

International Best-Selling Author of
Creating Your Own Destiny and *The Affluent Entrepreneur*

Introduction

YOU ARE NOT ALONE

"But sanctify the Lord God in your hearts: and be ready always to give an answer to every man that asketh you a reason of the hope that is in you with meekness and fear."

— 1 Peter 3:15

Nobody is perfect. We all make mistakes. My husband Max and I were working through some things in our marriage, and just when I thought things were getting better, we seemed to hit a wall. Until then, I could see and even feel the progress we were making as a couple with two young children. Lying in bed one night, I asked, no I begged, for him to tell me what he thought was keeping us from moving forward.

He finally said it. "I am in love with another woman." He felt relieved finally to say it out loud and get it off his chest. I felt crushed. Somehow, I slept that night. When I woke up the next morning, he had already left for work. I lay on the bed, thinking to myself, "What am I going to do? How will I move on from this?"

Two months earlier, I had been sitting in a church with 5,000 people on Easter Sunday. My neighbors and I had commuted together to church that day. My kids were in their Sunday school class and Max was in Australia. Despite being in a group of 5,000 people, I had never felt so alone in my life. I knew I could not keep up my life the way it was, trying to figure it all out on my own, so I decided to give up hope in my own strength and find a new hope. That was the day I gave my life over to Jesus. That day my loneliness changed somehow.

As I lay awake the morning after I learned Max was in love with another woman, I asked God, not really knowing how to pray or what to say, "Oh, Lord, how am I going to get through this pain?" I looked out the window with the curtains partially drawn, and I saw the shadow of a cross in the window as the sun came through. All I knew at that point was that I was not alone. God was with me, and just knowing He was there gave me the courage to get up and get moving.

Have you ever felt completely alone? Has your heart ever been broken? Have you ever felt so depressed that you could not get out of bed and move on with your day? If the answer to any of these questions is "Yes," then this book is for you. *The Hope Factor* is your solution and your roadmap to a new perspective on life.

One thing I have learned about myself is that I feel good when I feel understood. I can't say I know exactly what trials you are going through or how you feel, but I can tell you that I know how I felt when someone betrayed my trust, when I felt alone with no hope, when I was misunderstood, and when I continued to carry those hurts into all of my relationships. Maybe you are going through a divorce, or the death of a loved one, or discovering that your pain is so deep that you do not believe anyone or anything can soothe it. You are not alone. I wrote this book to offer help.

You may have noticed the pie dish on this book's cover and wondered about the meaning behind it. When I decided to write a book, I knew it had to be about hope and about being victorious and overcoming adversities in life. The book's title also came to me very quickly. With a title like *The Hope Factor*, and after filling this book with stories of victory and hope, I thought describing what hope is would be as easy as pie for me, but when I tried to describe hope, I found I needed to eat some humble pie because I realized I was wrong. It was not easy at all to describe hope in words or to describe what I felt in my heart. What seemed in the beginning to be a pie in the sky endeavor became less daunting from a different perspective when I examined hope one slice of pie at a time. It was only when I looked at each slice individually that I was able to put all the pieces together, and then what seemed so difficult to describe became very clear.

I do not know about you, but I learn a topic or receive a message best with stories and pictures to illustrate it. They help me remember what I have learned so I can recall it later and apply it to my life. When I can successfully learn new information and concepts, I get to grow and change, and I become stretched to new heights. This process is not always comfortable, but it is worth it.

In *The Hope Factor*, the idea of hope is broken down into five pieces of a pie. As you go through each chapter, you will be introduced to a slice of pie and the stories included with that piece will bring you to a place of understanding the meaning of hope. Exercises and questions throughout the book will help guide and assist you in your own process of self-discovery of what hope is in your life.

One of the basic premises to finding hope is knowing what the problem, trial, or circumstance is that is in need of a solution. Hope is *the* solution! It could be spiritual hope that you seek, or it could be the hope that you will solve a health issue, a relationship issue, a work issue, or some other problem.

Despite this entire book being about hope, there is still much to learn. Hope is a topic that is broad and deep and definitely a topic worth exploring for a lifetime. For the sake of discussion, let's divide people into two age groups: those under fifty years old and those over fifty years old. It would be safe to say that people over the age of fifty have had considerable life experiences, probably both good and bad, and they have had enough time also to sift through the baggage that may have accumulated over this time frame.

As a teacher of elementary and middle school students, starting at the age of twenty-one, and then doing a lot of substituting as Max and I moved to several cities, I had a plethora of experiences with different cultures and age groups. As Max and I began to have children, I eventually decided to be a stay-at-home mom. When my children were older, I eased back into the workforce as a pre-school teacher and a school bus driver, and later, I worked with high school youth groups and taught adult classes. I also had the joy of spending a few years working with the senior population and in healthcare. No matter where I found myself on my path or what age group I spent time or worked with, I always learned something from those around me.

Each age group brings me joy and hope, and I have heard stories from all of them that have brought me to tears of sadness and despair. As a teacher and a lifelong learner, my goal is to give you, the reader, hope. In doing so, I am rewarded tenfold on my own journey.

I know sometimes it can be hard to look at our pain head-on to move ahead. Discovering your hope will not make all of your troubles disappear, but gaining hope and allowing the light that comes with that hope to remove the darkness is a journey well worth the challenge, and I will be here to help.

As you read this book, I want you to know you are not alone. I have prayed for you before you even picked up this book. I have prayed that anyone reading this book in part or whole, alone or in a group, will discover the light through his or her pain. I pray you will embrace *Hope*.

Are you ready to begin? Are you ready to have your mind, body, soul, and spirit be stretched to a place of new understanding? Let's lock arms and take this journey together. You are not alone!

Full of Hope,

Sue Mocker

Sue Mocker

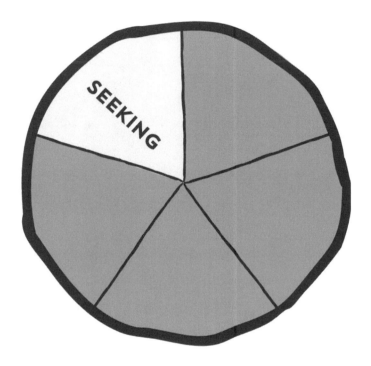

Seeking: To attempt to locate, discover, or search for; to endeavor to obtain or reach; to move toward.

Chapter One

COMMUNICATING HOPE

"Hope will never be silent."

— **Harvey Milk**

WHAT IS HOPE?

What is hope? How do you describe hope? What does hope mean for you? Many paths can lead to the finding and the feeling of hope. The actual definition of hope is to place confidence; to trust with confident expectation of good; or to cherish a desire of good. But *The Hope Factor* isn't about defining one specific meaning for hope. While I believe there is one hope, and for me it is Jesus Christ, many opportunities exist to seek out and find hope, and many people are ready to offer it. This book is not for Christians; it is for humans. Hope is big! Hope is universal, and hope is the one thing we *all* need.

The amazing Martin Luther King, Jr. gave hope to millions when he declared that he had a dream, when he bravely shared his vision and his message of hope with the world. Parents give hope to their children, leaders give hope to their followers, and businesses give hope to their employees and customers. Hope in so many forms is woven through every thread of society. Hope is necessary in every environment: work, home, relationships, and even leadership and business. Because hope is something we all need, how can we as a community and a culture begin to communicate about hope, its meaning and importance, unashamedly and boldly? How can we purposefully begin to communicate in a way that promotes and supports hope in all areas of our lives?

What if you have experienced what it feels like to be utterly hopeless? What if you are one of the many people in the world who has experienced indescribable adversity such as physical or sexual abuse, severe poverty, or addiction? How is it that some people are able to sustain incredible tragedy or abuses and to carry on normal lives, while others succumb to the horrors of their circumstances and become incapacitated and unable to function?

Resiliency is the ability to overcome problems, crises, and trauma, and to gain experience and wisdom as a direct result. Many current studies indicate that traumatic experiences, especially those experienced in childhood, increase difficulty in resiliency skills. These traumatic experiences include sexual abuse, physical abuse, and emotional abuse, including neglect. The more these factors are experienced, the higher the inability for a person to cope and the lower his or her resiliency.

I want to take a moment to explain the symptoms of emotional abuse because I believe emotional abuse can be covert and subtle; many people may not even realize they have been or are being emotionally abused in some way. Emotional abuse cuts deep to the core of a human being, and just because it does not leave a visible scar or is not a punch, kick, or hit, does not mean it is not abuse. Make no mistake about it; emotional abuse is just as damaging as any other kind of abuse. Some symptoms of emotional abuse include:

- Humiliation, degradation, discounting, negating, judging, criticizing

- Domination, control, shame

- Accusing, blaming, trivial and unreasonable demands or expectations, denying one's own shortcomings

- Emotional distancing, the "silent treatment," isolation, emotional abandonment, neglect

- Withholding basic needs (food, shelter, clothing) and/or money

It is important to identify whether or not you are being emotionally abused. If you are, get some help. Even if you think you *might* be experiencing emotional abuse, or if you identify with only one or two of the above symptoms, get help. Getting help can assist you in problem-solving solutions and give you a supportive outlet to heal.

Life has its share of difficulties for everyone, and at different points in our lives, we are presented with curveballs, sometimes big ones, which we never anticipated and which can take us to our knees. During such times, you can do some of the following specific strategies to bounce back and to use your experiences as "tools for growth":

- Affirm your strengths. Verbally and in your head, acknowledge your ability to overcome your challenges. When you find yourself feeling powerless, remind yourself that you can handle the situation. Speak words that support this positive and affirming mindset.

- Take whatever positive action you can to resolve the problem. Do not allow yourself to be incapacitated or immobilized by the situation. Instead, do what you can to resolve it so you feel accomplished rather than defeated.

- Get help and support from a friend. There is nothing as great as having a listening ear when you are trying to process through a difficult situation. Not only do you not have to go through crises alone, but by letting someone else be available for you, you may be contributing to his or her self-worth by making the person feel empowered and helpful.

- Be gentle and patient with yourself. There is a learning curve when coping with any new and uncharted challenge so cut yourself some slack! Affirm your strengths again and again and keep moving forward.

- Practice self-care. When things get difficult, give yourself the gifts of plenty of rest, good healthy food, exercise, prayer, and meditation.

These simple and effective tools will help you to stay positive and continue looking forward to your future. The way you handle your challenges will affect your ability to feel hopeful and to communicate hope even when you are going through personal challenges.

Exercise:

Reflect on the following questions:

When in your life have you had a sense of hopelessness? What were some of the circumstances that led to that feeling?

_____

_____

_____

_____

_____

How did these experiences affect your ability to be hopeful?

_____

_____

_____

_____

How did you behave in response to these experiences of hopeless-ness? How did you cope with your feelings at the time?

_____

_____

_____

_____

_____

Are there people in your life who have given you hope? Who are they and how did they help you?

_____

_____

_____

_____

_____

Do you have characteristics that can give hope to others? What are those characteristics and how can you contribute to someone else's ability to experience hope?

_____

_____

_____

_____

_____

Which of the "tools for growth" can you use to help you cope when you have difficult challenges in your life?

———————————————————————————————————

———————————————————————————————————

———————————————————————————————————

———————————————————————————————————

SECRETS: THE TRUTH SHALL SET YOU FREE

"And ye shall know the truth, and the truth shall make you free."

— John 8:32

So what makes me an expert on hope anyway? It is through the overcoming of my own experiences with adversity and feeling hopeless that I have been able to cultivate hope and make it the foundation of my life, and as a result, I have been able to share hope with many, many others. While this book is not about me and is not a memoir, I will share my personal experiences and background in a general way as a reference point for further insights and discussions found later in this book.

I was lonely as a child despite having two brothers and two sisters. I was also a Girl Scout, but I did not seem to relate well with the other kids. I was often teased and bullied and lacked the strength and coping skills to stand up for myself. I felt left out and powerless the majority of my childhood, but there were other things, secret things, going on that I dared not tell to anyone. I was disconnected from my family because it did not feel safe to tell them what was happening to me. I was alone and had to stuff my feelings down deep just to function.

I am the middle child of five children, and when I was about four years old, a distant family member, who unfortunately lived with us for several years, began coming to my bedroom, waking me up, and taking me to his bedroom. This started to happen often, though I do not recall how many nights a week. For a duration of somewhere between five and six years, I was molested. I remember thinking at the time that I must be so lucky to have been chosen to be with him. His bedroom was not the only place in the house we would go for privacy. I have very few memories of my childhood prior to sixth grade and I know I blocked them out because I was molested. When I began the sixth grade, the molestation ceased because the family member abusing me moved out.

I had no memories of being molested until I was twenty-nine years old. Later, I was diagnosed with PTSD (post-traumatic stress disorder), which explained my failure to remember the abuse. Once I began having memories, the abuse explained so much about why I had thought and acted the way I did in my adult life up until that point. I have experienced many challenges in my life that I believe are a direct result of being molested, including:

- Feeling compelled as an adult to keep secrets. I have had difficulty discussing or being open about things that do not feel right in my gut or things I need to address when I believe there is something important I need to communicate to someone.

- I have been fearful when I get woken up in the middle of the night by sounds or people. When my children came to me in the middle of the night, the sound of their movement in the hall reminded me of my abuser coming down the hall to get me.

- It bothers me when someone holds my wrists in certain ways. I believe it was because I was held down by my wrists.

- I have trouble taking baths. I have memories of something happening in the bathtub, though I am not clear about what happened.

- I am very scared when people try to scare me on purpose, even in jest.

- I do not like to become sweaty when working out or in hot weather.

- I have struggled with standing up for myself when involved with controlling or overbearing people, and I have felt as if I have to go along with someone or something bad might happen to me.

With help from counseling over the years, I have been able to heal from most of these responses, thoughts, and feelings, but some still linger. Knowing now where these responses, thoughts, and feelings originated has lessened my fear and has created an emotional safety net for me.

Equally as cathartic was my relationship with my first love and husband, Max. He and I began dating when I was fifteen years old. We fell in love according to what I thought love was supposed to be. We both decided that having our college degrees was a priority and would need to be accomplished before we got married, so we had plenty of time to date each other. We worked at the same Wendy's fast-food restaurant in high school and during the first couple of years of college.

One day, one of my fellow female employees came to work with a hickey on her neck. I was informed by someone that my boyfriend Max had given her the hickey while having sex with her in a hotel room. I left work that day crying and devastated. I was a senior in high school at the time, and I had a few long research papers to write, but I had a horrible time trying to concentrate on my homework. It took me a couple of days just to get a handle on my emotions. I was able to get needed support from my mother, and I believed my relationship with Max would now end. After all, how could he have done this to me and to us?

Max responded to the situation by telling me he loved me, wanted to marry me, and did not want to lose me, and I believed he meant it. He also said he had made the choice to be with the other girl because he wanted to experience what it would be like to have sex with someone else *before* we got married because once we got married, I would be his one and only love. I believed him and eventually forgave him. I did not know at the time that I deserved to be treated better because I really had nothing else with which to compare our relationship.

After we graduated from college, we got married just as we had planned. I had always daydreamed about marriage and imagined it would be a mutually intimate partnership, but for me, it felt like I was responsible for satisfying someone else's needs and that my needs were irrelevant.

In the meantime, our married life together began to evolve with the birth of our first daughter, Lindsey. On the day she was born, we found out she had a severe medical condition, called total anomalous pulmonary venous connection! What did that even mean? I was numb and in disbelief about what the doctors were trying to explain to me. My daughter was born with a congenital heart defect that left her with no oxygenated blood going back to her heart, and she would need to be transferred to the Children's Hospital. Without open-heart surgery, Lindsey would die within seven days.

When the doctors spoke to us about Lindsey's chance of living, they said she had a 20 percent chance to survive through the surgery. Her heart condition was rare, but they assured me that she was in the hospital best able to help her. I really did not know what strength I had inside of me, but I believed that my daughter would live. I remember trying to fall asleep while still in the hospital, knowing all the while that my daughter was not there with me.

When I woke up, Max was sleeping on the couch in my room and my two sisters were sitting on the floor waiting to help in whatever way they could. They had driven all the way from out of state, one from Iowa, and the other from Nebraska. With their presence, I was suddenly faced with the reality of the situation and began to cry uncontrollably. I thought about how special my sisters were to come to support me. I did not realize the true gravity of Lindsey's condition, and unbeknown to me, all my family members were either on their way or trying to get there, fearing the worst.

Our daughter was the first grandchild on Max's side of the family and the third on mine. I was only twenty-four years old, but I was on a journey that would take me places I didn't know I needed to go. My denial was so strong that I was thinking, "Why is everyone coming to see us? She is having open heart surgery at two days old, but I'm sure she will be okay." When I was discharged from the hospital, I was able to visit Lindsey at The Children's Hospital Intensive Care Unit (ICU). Despite the oxygen tank, she looked fine and normal.

The nurses quietly and gently began preparing me for what was to come and my daughter's chances for survival— 20 percent, they affirmed. Of course, we called the whole family to tell them the news and that the surgery would take place in twelve hours. At first, Max did not inform his parents because he did not want to admit to himself or his parents that his daughter "came out" imperfect. How could he have created an "imperfect" child? He finally did call them and they said they could not get a plane so they would have to drive. Max's parents began the eleven-hour drive to head our way. Within several hours, my family also started arriving both to meet and say goodbye to my daughter.

However, things are rarely what they seem. In one of the most difficult times of my life, what I was privately thinking about was my secret. I wondered whether my baby's illness was God's way of punishing me for something I had done when I was seventeen. I kept thinking to myself, "Surely God is not the kind of God who would punish my child for something I did to get back at *me*." She was an innocent child after all and had done nothing wrong. But I had done something very bad; in fact, it was unmentionable, and I could not talk to anyone about it because I was too ashamed.

I went to see Lindsey one last time before surgery, and one nurse in particular spoke to me again about her chances of living, but for the first time, I got a different answer. This nurse said so confidently that I need not worry about my daughter's chances to live and to think about it like this: "Your daughter has a 100 percent chance to live, or a 100 percent chance to die. We don't know the outcome, but God does."

Somehow, this thought gave me comfort, though it again brought up the question about whether God would allow my daughter to die because of my secret sin. I had grown up Catholic and had gone to confession, although not very often. After my "big sin," I went to confession because I thought if I told the priest about it, he would surely let me off the hook. I always thought the priest would forgive my sin if I were honest. I thought that if I confessed what I did, he would give me a few prayers to say, and then I would go kneel in the pew and say the prayers and that would be that.

I could not bring myself to tell the priest what I actually did, so I said something that would give him a clue so he would hopefully figure it out. He gave me several hundred prayers to say. Now, I either heard him wrong, or he figured out I did something very bad. Either way, I said all the prayers with the hope that my sin would be forgiven and forgotten.

But at twenty-four years old, with a new baby going into surgery, it was not forgotten, and at this point, I didn't believe I was forgiven. I questioned whether my daughter's medical condition was God's way of punishing me. Why couldn't I tell anyone? I had never felt so alone, so desolate in all of my life.

You see, Max and I had dated from the time I was fifteen and he was sixteen. He was my first boyfriend and we stayed a couple, all the way through college until we both graduated. We were engaged and then married in early 1985. When we were seventeen, and sexually active, I had become pregnant. At that time, it seemed as if the only answer was to have an abortion. We did not tell our parents or anyone; we just figured out how to make it go away. I was so afraid, and saying a bunch of prayers did not take away the guilt and shame of our decision, but at least no one knew, at least that is what I thought. There would never be a reason for it ever to be talked about or brought up again.

The time came for Lindsey's surgery and we kissed her goodbye. I cried as they wheeled her off and Max and I were escorted into the waiting area in the back. The "Do Not Enter" doors burst open with one set of running grandparents, and it occurred to me that, until then, I had forgotten my husband's parents had not arrived. Their drive was eleven hours, but somehow they made it in nine. They wanted to see their grandbaby alive, maybe for the last time. They were crying as well, but they were able to see my daughter just in time before her surgery. The nurses told us how fortunate we were to have the greatest surgeon, and I trusted them when they told me this. I waited and I trusted. I received a call from my brother who was unable to come, and he assured me everything would be okay. Somehow, instinctively, I knew he was right.

That was the longest night of my life, but my daughter survived. A few hours after surgery, cheering was heard in the ICU. Lindsey's blood oxygen levels had stabilized and she was now out of the woods and moving toward recovery. Miraculously, six days later, we were able to take her home. For seven years after her surgery, my daughter was under the watchful eye of both the doctors and her parents as we anxiously waited for the day when she would grow into a healthy child, and surely, she did. God had not forsaken me; He had not punished my daughter for something I had done. He had forgiven me, and now I knew I was responsible to do the work necessary to begin the healing process. I needed to take a hard look at what was in my heart. Little did I know that would take many years as I pushed it into my past, believing it was over, and not realizing I was changed forever by that decision.

Seven years into my marriage to Max, I began to have memories of my childhood sexual abuse. By this time, I had given birth to my second daughter and had experienced considerable female health problems. Max had blamed me all along for our first daughter's heart condition. His attitude was very hurtful and created even more distance in our relationship. At the time, I was taking care of two babies, doing my best to take care of myself, and trying to cope with our marital problems. We attended counseling, which helped somewhat, but a constant undertow in my heart made me feel something was not right. Our marriage seemed to lack closeness, true intimacy, but I could not put my finger on exactly what was wrong.

The more I began to experience the memories and feelings of being abused, the less sexually responsive I became. I tried to show my husband I loved him in other ways, but he had checked out emotionally. I began my own journey through church and counseling, I started healing from the effects of the trauma and abuse I had experienced, and I finally started to understand what had been wrong all along. I also knew that I had the potential to be unreasonably demanding and emotional. Max had every right to be upset and emotionally detached to some degree, but I also discovered that what I had truly been lacking was knowing that I was loved by God. Once I came to know and accept God's love, I realized what love *really* is, and I was able to practice my newfound principles of love in my marriage.

The feelings of anger I experienced from my childhood abuse began to dissipate, and I was able to forgive the perpetrator for what he did to me. I thought I could finally move forward in my marriage, and I thought that because Max and I were going to church together, our marriage would change for the better, but this was not the case. Max confessed that he was in love with another woman. Despite this challenge, both Max and I decided we wanted to try to make our marriage work, especially for our two young children. Once again, I was able with grace from God to forgive my husband.

Max and I started learning how to love each other again, and as a result, we became a strong couple; only this time, our relationship was even better because we were both learning the love of God—how much He loved us, and how much more we could love each other and our children. Many years passed, and in the year 2000, we moved from the Midwest to the Seattle area. It *seemed* we had guarded our marriage so carefully after all we had been through together as a couple, and as a family, that we had finally gotten to a great place in our marriage. We began to lead the youth group at our church, and on the outside, everything appeared okay, but I began to notice behavior changes in my husband.

Max traveled a lot, and it seemed often that on the day he was scheduled to come home, he would change his return day and come home a day later than planned. He always had a convincing story about why he had to change the date, but then he would return home angry, as if something were really bothering him. Max began missing the days he was supposed to teach the Bible lesson at church because of these extended business trips, stating that he just "didn't have adequate time to prepare" for the lesson. This seemed strange to me. I took responsibility for covering his classes, but I knew something was not right. He denied that anything was going on, and he kept coming up with excuses that sounded fairly reasonable to me.

Seven years later, our marriage seriously began to suffer again. Our girls had grown up and moved on, and I wondered whether their absence was affecting Max because he was very attached to our daughters. Then in 2007, it became clear that Max was not being honest. His business trips continued, and his phone calls home at night became inconsistent. In December of 2007, he announced that he wanted a divorce. He told me he did not love me and never had. Max denied having an affair, even after he was caught going out with another woman by a mutual friend. I could no longer tolerate the dishonesty and deceit.

I was devastated beyond words, but I agreed to the divorce. The ending of our marriage affected me emotionally and physically. I later found out that Max had been having affairs all along from the time we began dating until he asked for a divorce. I did not understand how my husband could make a covenant of love to me and behave in the ways he had. I know now that the love we had was toxic, and while in my gut I had often felt it over the course of our marriage, I was unable to understand it.

There had been other secrets along the way, but not all secrets are damaging. Consider a surprise party where a secret is kept to create a positive outcome. Some secrets can be harmless and even healthy. Young adolescents learn about their identities by keeping some information private. On the other hand, my secrets kept me sick and in bondage, and until I actually began to share my secrets with God and another human being, my secrets ruled my life. Despite the horror and devastation I experienced when the truth about my sexual abuse and marriage came to light, indeed, the truth has set me free.

Gloria Estefan's song "Coming Out of the Dark" eloquently describes the restoration from unhealthy and toxic love to the mighty love that I have found in my God and in myself. In this song, she asks why she should be afraid if she is not alone. She questions her beliefs, only to find that once coming out of the dark, nothing is really written in stone and the sun is shining on her. She begins to understand that even though she is starting over and it may still be a long painful road, she stands on the rock that is the love of God and that His love has helped her all the way from the dark into the light. You see, God knows you by name. Isaiah 43:1 states:

> *"But now thus sayeth the LORD that created thee, O Jacob, and he that formed thee, O Israel, Fear not: for I have redeemed thee, I have called thee by thy name; thou art mine."*

I am also reminded by the song "Coming Out of the Dark" that some people never realize they have been in the dark because they have never experienced standing in the light. This was the case for me as well. When you do not share your secrets and are holding back due to fear or shame or not wanting to hurt other people, you are still in the dark.

For example, when I began speaking the truth about my sexual abuse, some of my relatives became fearful that the truth would hurt other family members. While it is true that people may be hurt by the truth, on the opposite side of the coin, denying the truth or hiding the truth could deprive these same people of healing. When I was finally brave enough to tell my family about being sexually abused, I gained healing support from them and they were able to gain valuable clarity, healing, and understanding. They finally understood many of the ways I responded while growing up that did not make sense until they knew about the abuse.

Keeping secrets can take a heavy toll on the body, mind, and spirit. Some scientific studies indicate that people who have a tendency to conceal or withhold information over time can experience anxiety, depression, and overall body aches and pains. Anita Kelly, a Doctor of Psychology at the University of Notre Dame, has studied how keeping secrets affects the body. She says, "Quite simply … secretive people also tend to be sick people … I don't think it's much of a stretch to say that being secretive could be linked to being symptomatic at a biological level."

Keeping secrets can also become all-consuming because it takes a lot of work and energy to maintain a secret. So which is healthier: Keeping a secret that causes strain on you, or telling the truth, which may hurt you and others and create discomfort? Only you can make that decision, but here are some things to consider when deciding whether or not to talk about a secret:

- Certain secrets are only between you and God because they are special and private.

- Certain secrets should not be told or must be told only in a safe environment because they can put you or others in physical danger.

- Certain secrets must be told because not telling them may support behaviors that continue to harm you or others.

It is important to be mindful about how, when, and even whether to share secrets. For instance, it would not be appropriate to share your secret during a wedding, funeral, or some other milestone event because doing so could cause a lasting or traumatic negative impact. Keep in mind that sharing a secret, despite the freedom that may accompany your confession, will most likely influence those around you. It would be helpful ahead of time to think through your confession and the impact it may have on others. Letting our secrets out has definite benefits, but also definite consequences. If your secret is a fantastic surprise, by all means, go for it, but for deeper and graver secrets, make sure you have a post-secret action plan and are prepared to cope with the responses of others, whatever those responses may be.

Remember that confessing your secrets can be really scary, but the advantage is that you will be free to communicate in a way that is truthful and that will allow you to live in reality rather than in denial. When I experienced and understood this truth for myself, I was, indeed, set free.

Exercise:

Here are some questions for reflection:

Are you keeping a secret that is causing you or someone else physical, emotional, and/or spiritual harm? What kind of secret?

_____

_____

_____

_____

_____

Would telling your secret hurt anyone else? How so?

_____

_____

_____

_____

_____

What is the benefit of keeping the secret? What is the payoff?

_____

_____

_____

_____

What would be the benefit of confessing the secret? What would be the payoff?

_____

_____

_____

_____

If you are considering confessing your secret, whom would you tell and what would your action plan be to cope with others' responses?

_____

_____

_____

_____

_____

Only you can decide whether you need to bring your secrets out into the light of day. Be sure to pray, to examine all the angles, and to be aware of the pros and cons of both telling the secret and keeping the secret before you make a decision. One thing is for sure: the truth can set you free.

COMMUNICATING HOPE

At home, at work, everywhere you go, and every place you spend your time, you are communicating through the use of language, both bodily and through words. Your words can be an elixir or they can be poison. They can build up both you and those around you, or they can cut you all down. With the words you speak, you choose whether you will hurt or whether you will heal. What message are you sending through your use of words? Are you supporting and promoting hope or do your words contribute to hopelessness?

First impressions are made in seconds. When you meet someone, look him or her in the face and say, "It is a pleasure to meet you" because even the word "pleasure" opens up your mouth to look like a smile, and you are then sending out positive healing energy. Good energy is something everyone wants! The opposite is also true. If you meet someone and do not make eye contact, if you do not acknowledge that person in a positive way or express any interest in him or her, you will typically send out negative energy that can naturally repel people from you.

Communication is about perception, not intention. If you are dragging around all the junk in your trunk, telling everyone how miserable you are, speaking negatively, or complaining all the time, what kind of effect do you think that will have on those around you? Do you want to be around someone like that? Probably not for any length of time! Here is a quick and fun experiment:

First, go stand in front of a mirror. Then wrinkle your forehead as if you are angry or unhappy and try to smile at the same time!

It looks quite strange, doesn't it?

A SOFT ANSWER TURNS AWAY WRATH

A good friend of mine told me a story about the value of compassion and responding with a soft answer. She said that when her children were small, she rarely got the opportunity to sleep in, so she decided she would empower her older son to make cereal for his younger sibling in the morning so she could sleep in for once. That evening, she described to her older son in a general way what he needed to do to prepare breakfast in the morning for himself and his younger brother.

Her older son was only four or five years old at the time, but he thought this was a fantastic idea, and he was willing and ready to take on the responsibility of making breakfast the following morning. While my friend slept in, he did, indeed, make breakfast for himself and his younger sibling.

Upon awakening, my friend went downstairs to discover that only one bowl of cereal had been eaten and the other remained full and soggy on the dining room table. She became infuriated that her older son would waste all that milk and cereal. She began yelling and ranting at him about being wasteful and he became upset.

Through his tears, he explained to her that he did not eat his cereal because by the time he was able to go through the process of making cereal for his little brother, his cereal became gross and soggy. Looking at her crying son, she realized that her expectations had been unrealistic, and in part, she had expected him to do something without completely explaining how it should be done. She felt horrible for getting so angry when what her young son needed was understanding and more specific and clear direction. She learned a big lesson that day.

A soft answer means practicing anger control. You will find that if you literally practice compassion in your voice and speak softly, especially when you are upset, you will experience the best outcome and responses from others. For instance, even during an argument in the heat of the moment, if you remain calm and use compassion in your voice, you will find that you begin to de-escalate not only yourself, but also the entire situation. While other people may get angry with you because you are so calm and will not engage with them, you will have satisfaction and peace of mind from knowing that you did not engage with them out of anger.

Anger is like a dance between two people. The angry energy is transferred from one person to another, but if one person stops dancing, it leaves the other person to dance alone. It is no fun to dance alone, and the person who continues dancing will do one of two things: He will eventually quit dancing, or he will go find someone else with whom to do the anger dance.

It can also be very helpful to understand your own body language in relation to anger because the earlier you can identify your anger, the easier it will be to keep it from escalating or to deter it altogether. If you can begin to feel anger in your body, you can head it off at the pass before you react. While anger symptoms vary from person to person, here are some of the more common ones that occur in our bodies when we begin to experience anger:

- Grinding or clenching teeth
- Clenching fists
- Flushed skin or prickly sensations
- Sweating
- Muscle tension
- Body temperature changes

"A soft answer turneth away wrath:
but grievous words stir up anger."

— Proverbs 15:1

This advice means that kindness produces kindness, and in turn, rage produces rage. To have compassion means you have empathy for others' suffering. When people act out in anger, they are suffering, so what can you do to provide a soft answer?

Exercise:

Reflect on the following questions:

What is an example of a time when you responded out of anger rather than with a soft answer? What was the outcome?

_____

_____

_____

_____

What is an example of a time when you responded with a soft answer? What was the outcome?

_____

_____

_____

_____

What is the value to your mind, body, and spirit in responding with softness rather than anger?

_____

_____

_____

_____

With which of the symptoms that described anger in the body did you identify? How do you know in _your_ body when you are beginning to get angry?

_____

_____

_____

_____

What are some actions you can take to diffuse your anger before it gets out of control?

_____

_____

_____

_____

_____

Always keep in mind that you catch more flies with honey than vinegar every time. You have the choice to respond with love and compassion rather than anger.

LONELINESS AMONG THE MASSES

When I was going through my very painful divorce, I could sit in a room full of people and feel completely alone. At work, in church, everywhere, I had a sense that I was completely disconnected. For me, this feeling was very familiar, and in my heart was the same feeling I had experienced when I was growing up. The truth is that I had felt alone my entire life. I was horribly lonely as a child, despite having siblings and being involved in activities.

A while back, I was involved with a family who nicknamed one of their children "Lardo" because he was very overweight. I wondered whether it hurt him that his own family would call him by such a derogatory nickname. I can personally relate to how he must have felt, and I believe today that the reason why I am so compassionate and in tune with others' feelings is because of how I was treated by the mean kids growing up.

When I was small, I often wondered what the other children were coping with at their homes, those things they were not allowed to talk about. I also had compassion for others who were being bullied and teased because I knew firsthand how that felt.

An echo occurs when one is subjected to mistreatment, and the echo is long lasting and reaches far into the depths of our spirits. We carry this echo, this loneliness, with us into our adulthoods. My hope is that if you are someone like me who has experienced loneliness that goes deep to your core, to your very spirit, that you will be able to find your own healing and step into the light.

To finish Lardo's story, at one point I heard him referring to *himself* as Lardo, and he seemed quite fine with the nickname at that moment. Maybe for him it was a term of endearment that he felt good about, but it still seemed mean to me. This is another great example of how words can be used to hurt or heal. Use your words wisely and make sure you know to whom you are talking before you designate someone *as* something or assume words are not hurtful. Was Lardo just poking fun at himself because everyone else did, or was his own use of his nickname just a cover in order to cope? Had he begun to believe the negative way others saw him was the truth about who he was? I may never know, but the lesson for me is to be compassionate to the best of my ability.

While the term "loneliness" describes a state of being alone or in solitude, loneliness can also be a state of mind. For instance, people who feel empty, alone, and unwanted can become depressed and have difficulty forming relationships with others as a result. Loneliness is, in fact, the perception that you are alone, which may not necessarily be true, but it sure feels true in the moment.

What actually contributes to feelings of loneliness? Here are some common variables that create the feeling of loneliness:

- Keeping secrets
- Moving to a new place (physically, mentally, or spiritually)
- Divorce
- Job change
- Death of a significant person or a pet
- A psychological or physical disorder such as depression or menopause
- Low self-esteem

Maybe you can add to the list. I feel I would be remiss if I did not mention isolation from others as a contributor to loneliness. In my opinion, isolation from others has been significantly exacerbated by the increased use of the Internet and other social electronic media, resulting in a decrease in actual face-to-face relationship building. I wonder what the long-term effects will be on intimacy and relationships and our ability to connect truly with one another when our society is currently so focused on computer relationships and social media.

Loneliness has also been linked to health risks including:

- Depression and suicide
- Increased stress levels
- Cardiovascular disease and stroke
- Decreased memory
- Poor decision-making
- Increased use of alcohol and other drugs

Loneliness is not exclusive to the United States. People around the world experience loneliness. Be mindful, be helpful, and be supportive. Practice compassion in all areas of your life: at home, at work, and in your relationships. Be the one person someone may have in his or her life who really cares. When you find yourself struggling with feelings of loneliness, try using the Ten Tools to Combat Loneliness:

TEN TOOLS TO COMBAT LONELINESS

1. Call a friend and share your feelings. Getting your feelings out often provides immediate relief and gives someone else the opportunity to be helpful.

2. Take a walk or do some sort of physical exercise. Not only does physical exercise relieve stress on the body, but it also promotes clarity of the mind and affects the "feel good" neurotransmitters in the brain.

3. Do some writing; journaling can be a cathartic tool, and there is something that happens between the heart and the pen that does not always happen between the mind and the mouth.

4. Listen to uplifting music.

5. Find a hobby or a craft that brings you joy.

6. Seek support via a community or church group.

7. When all else fails, help someone else. Helping others gets you out of yourself and you may even forget you were lonely in the first place.

8. Pray. Get plugged in and connected to God in the way that works best for you.

9.   Spend time in nature. Go to a park, on a hike, or anywhere you can see, feel, and experience nature.

10.   Practice good self-care. Eat healthy, get enough rest, and make sure you are doing what you need to be good to yourself.

Mix and match these tools and share them with others. In my darkest hour, when I was going through my divorce and was so indescribably lonely, I was blessed to have the support of my beautiful daughters and, above all, God—they all became my biggest cheerleaders. As my relationship with God continued to flower and grow, I became so much better and stronger, and I was delivered from the dark to the light.

Exercise:

Has loneliness affected your body, mind, or spirit? How?

_____

_____

_____

_____

_____

_____

What have you done in the past to cope with feelings of loneliness, and how did that work for you?

_____

_____

_____

_____

Which of the Ten Tools to Combat Loneliness would you be willing to try next time you are feeling lonely?

_____

_____

_____

_____

_____

_____

Who is one person you can call when you are feeling lonely?

_____

_____

_____

How has God been there for you in your life, and how can He help you in your times of difficulty?

_____

_____

_____

_____

_____

_____

_____

_____

_____

My beautiful daughter Lindsey wrote a song that touched my heart and really exemplified the way I felt during the darkest times I have experienced in my life. Maybe you, too, can relate to it and find comfort through its message of hope.

Hopelessness Fades
by Lindsey Larson

I was sitting down

With my head cast down

My cheeks were stained with tears

And I was feeling hopeless

But then I looked up and over

And through the window glass

I saw birds eating in the grass

And You whispered to my soul

Chorus

I take care of the birds

Why wouldn't I take care of you?

I take care of the birds

Why wouldn't I take care of you?

You're my precious daughter

You're made in my likeness

You're my precious daughter

You're made with a purpose

Then my phone rang

And it was a friend

Pretending nothing's wrong

I just hid my pain

Then she asked me over for dinner

Thankful I said, "Yes"

I was feeling much less stress

And You whispered to my soul

Chorus

I take care of the birds

Why wouldn't I take care of you?

I take care of the birds

Why wouldn't I take care of you?

You're my precious daughter

You're made in my likeness

You're my precious daughter

You're made with a purpose

Reminded of the Truth

My LORD provided

Delighted in my soul

I was feeling grateful

And then I stood up and smiled

As hopelessness fades

My mind cleared from the haze

Now I whisper to your soul

Bridge

I dwell in Hope
Because of my Savior
(Repeat 4 times)

Now I share this Truth with you

Final Chorus

He takes care of the birds
And He will take care of you
He takes care of the birds
And He will take care of you
You're His precious daughter
You're made in His likeness
You're His precious daughter
You're made with a purpose

Now dwell in Hope

When I asked Lindsey why she wrote the song, she said, "The song is a true story about how God comforted me when I was feeling hopeless. I want everyone to know they are valuable, have a purpose, and that the Lord provides."

SUMMARY

People all over the world suffer from loneliness. You never know what challenges someone else may be facing. You never know what emotional load someone else may be carrying. Do your best to let each interaction you have with others lift them up and support them whenever possible. Remember that loneliness can affect your body, mind, and spirit, but there are tools you can pick up and use anytime to begin moving out of the darkness of loneliness. When you feel alone and you are hurting, you can *always* lean on God. He will always be there, and you are never really alone. Your feelings of hopelessness will indeed fade.

A TREASURE AND A PEARL

You may be *seeking* many things in your life at this time. Even if you aren't sure what you are seeking, if you open up, you will find answers to your questions and you may even find answers to questions you did not know you had. When I needed comfort, safety, and truth, I was invited to church. I needed freedom from my secrets and to find a cure for my loneliness. Church became my sanctuary, my lifeline, and the answer to the questions I had been asking for so long. What are *you* seeking?

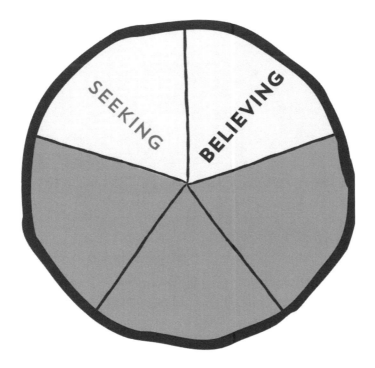

Believing: To accept something as true; feel sure of the truth.

Chapter Two

FINDING HOPE IN RELATIONSHIPS

"Treasure your relationships, not your possessions."

— **Anthony J. D'Angelo**

YOU ARE VALUABLE

Did you know that your thinking and the way you feel about yourself affects not only your choices but also your behavior? I believed in God from an early age, and I knew that He sent His Son to the cross, but I did not believe that He did that *for me*. I thought He sent His Son for *other* people, the ones who *deserved* His favor. Talk about lonely! I had serious conflict between the idea that God loves me and my own inability to be perfect, which is how I thought I was supposed to be in order to receive God's love.

I was also worried about how my religion would affect my relationship with God because I thought that being part of a church meant that I had to follow every rule perfectly or I would be "in trouble" or "condemned." I thought there was really nothing I could do "not" to be in trouble. After all, I knew I was imperfect, so I felt I was not good enough and never could be. If He did in fact die for me, it seemed embarrassing to come to this conclusion at the age of thirty because even little kids seem to know that Jesus died for their sins and they are loved by God. As an educator, should I not already know this?

Over time, I continued to learn about, practice, and share my beliefs with like-minded people. I began believing that maybe my life could improve, and maybe I was worthy and "enough" in God's eyes after all. As people started believing in me and asking to help me, and as I began accepting help and letting people into my heart, I began hearing a message that I could not hear before. I began to learn and hear that God *desires* to have a relationship with me and that Jesus died on the cross for *me*!

I had moments of disbelief as my faith continued to grow. One of my biggest challenges was understanding how God could possibly want a relationship with me when my own husband did not. Over time, I became aware of character qualities about a God I had never heard about before, and I began believing that God loved me and that I *was* loveable despite my brokenness and imperfection.

My self-worth and identity were based on being a wife up to that point, but I began to realize that my self-worth is really contingent upon living in truth, being myself, and acknowledging that I am a child of the King. I am a treasure and a pearl, and I am good enough! Whatever I do is my work on this earth, and my purpose includes helping and serving other people. Instead of pain, shame, and darkness, I am now walking in the light. I am connected and I have an ever-increasing connection with God, who is loving and mighty! Jude 22 says, "*And of some have compassion, making a difference.*" This is my mission: to have compassion and make a difference in the lives of those who need the light.

Exercise:

How do you feel about yourself? What are your character assets and positive qualities?

_____

_____

_____

_____

_____

How do you believe God sees you? Do you believe you are worthy of God's love?

_____

_____

_____

_____

_____

What could you do to increase and grow your relationship with God?

_____

_____

_____

_____

_____

Are there others in your life who may be able to help you on your journey? Who?

_____

_____

_____

_____

_____

Are there people in your life who need *your* help? Who are they and how can you help them now?

_____

_____

_____

_____

_____

_____

_____

If you are feeling like you are not worthy of God's love, I want you to know you are not alone. Even if you feel imperfect or unworthy, even if you have made big mistakes along the way, you are redeemed. You will find a strong enduring faith as you continue learning, connecting, and growing your spiritual relationship with God. One day, maybe even sooner than later, you will come to believe you *are* worthy, always have been worthy, and always will be worthy of God's love. God created you because He loves you and because He wants to be in a relationship with you. He has indeed loved you all along.

Recognize also that your self-worth is an inside job. No one has the power to affect your self-worth without your permission. When you begin feeling better about yourself, you will not allow others to have power over your self-worth anymore. You will need to dig deep, especially if you have experienced the kind of adversity that scars your soul. Emotional, physical, and sexual abuse, domestic violence, and other forms of adversity and abuse can have a permanent and lasting effect on our hearts.

As you develop a stronger and closer relationship with your Creator and with yourself, you will find He will give you the courage and grace to move forward on the path of discovery, which may feel scary at times.

Take whatever action you need to identify and acknowledge the good things about yourself. Learn to be your own best supporter. While we all need other people and no one lives life in a silo, *you* must make decisions and practice tools that contribute to your wellbeing. Here are some great tips for building positive esteem within yourself:

- Make sure you are speaking and thinking highly of yourself. Do not cut yourself down in front of others. When you find yourself thinking negative thoughts about yourself, interrupt the negative self-talk with positive self-talk. Declare something great about you. Look at your list of positive qualities and character attributes and say them aloud each day.

- Do not say, "Yes" when you mean "No." Doing things you do not want to do and putting yourself in situations that cause you stress, discomfort, and negative feelings can tear you down. Instead, practice saying, "No." Do your best to make commitments that support your wellbeing. Though in reality we all have to do things that do not feel good sometimes, overall you decide how to spend your time. Spend it wisely and positively!

- Spend time with God. Any relationship requires time, and that includes your special and personal relationship with God. Take the time each day to talk to and listen to God, pray, and worship—whatever that entails for you. When you are connected, plugged in, and spiritually fit, you will naturally feel better about yourself.

Exercise:

What is one action you can take each day that will contribute to your self-worth?

_____

_____

_____

_____

_____

What are some things you can say to yourself when you become aware that you are speaking or thinking unkind thoughts about yourself?

_____

_____

_____

_____

_____

Your unique relationship with God is like no other relationship because He loves you unconditionally. While this may be a new concept for you, God's love for you is not based on:

- Your good deeds or lack thereof
- Whether or not you feel you love Him enough or correctly
- Your ability to love Him or others
- Whether you believe you are unworthy or worthy
- Your height, weight, ethnicity, or any other physical or cultural characteristic
- Whether you feel broken or whole, imperfect or perfect

God loves you merely because God is love.

"In this was manifested the love of God toward us, because that God sent his only begotten Son into the world, that we might live through him. Herein is love, not that we loved God, but that he loved us, and sent his Son to be the propitiation for our sins."

— 1 John 4:9-10

There is nothing you could do, or fail to do, that would cause God to love you any less. You are *His* treasure and *His* pearl.

A TREASURE AND A PEARL

"A fine glass vase goes from treasure to trash, the moment it is broken. Fortunately, something else happens to you and me. Pick up your pieces. Then, help me gather mine."

— Vera Nazarian

Several of my friends were struggling in their marriages at the same time I found out that Max had been unfaithful throughout our marriage. As these women and I began sharing our stories and our deepest feelings about problems such as separation, divorce, and infidelity, I began noticing that many of them felt so defeated. One woman in particular remarked that at her age (close to fifty), she believed any further relationships would just consist of "trading in one problem for another." She also stated that she believed the "likelihood of meeting someone different is slim." I was surprised and saddened by this notion, and I quickly discovered I did not want to believe those negative thoughts! I was not willing to settle for someone who might treat me poorly. I made a decision at that very moment that if I were ever going to be with another man, I wanted to be treated like a treasure and a pearl. Without even knowing what that would feel like, I decided it was the only option.

Matthew 13:44-46 explains that God's kingdom is like finding a hidden treasure or a pearl of great value. This treasure is connected to our hearts, the place of desire and longing. I asked God with all of my heart to send someone to love me who could treat me like a hidden treasure and value me like a great pearl. I also asked wholeheartedly that He send me someone who had never been married and who had no children. I felt that my own girls had endured enough pain during my divorce, so I wanted to make sure they would not be hurt any further in my process of finding love again.

A few months later, while at church, I began noticing a man named Frank who mentioned he had never been married and had no children. We were on the same ministry team, and like others on my team, I treated him to a fruit smoothie as a small token of thanks. We had such a great time together that we decided to begin dating. While attending church together one Sunday, the pastor's sermon included the statement that Jesus treats us like a treasure and a pearl. To my surprise and utter delight, Frank, who was sitting directly beside me, leaned over and said, "That's how I want to treat you." I knew right away that he was the man for me and that God had given me the literal words through Frank that I needed to hear to make the decision to love again! Talk about a blessing! Frank and I are married now, and we have a great life together with God in the center.

We are all meant to lift each other up and to love one another unconditionally to the very best of our abilities. We all have talents and gifts that are God-given and inherent in our very make-up. God never makes mistakes. This is why it is our God-given responsibility to take measures to grow, change, and heal ourselves, and to help others along the way. We are all treasures and pearls.

A great E.E. Cummings quote states, *"It takes courage to grow up and become who you really are."* When you begin to realize and truly experience that you are God's handiwork, you will begin to see clearly that you are very special to God.

Exercise:

In what ways has God already blessed your life and revealed to you that you are His treasure and His pearl?

_____

_____

_____

_____

_____

What are your God-given talents and how can you share these with others?

_____

_____

_____

_____

_____

What action can you take to use these talents and to let others know they, too, are God's treasures and pearls?

_____

_____

_____

_____

_____

At the end of each chapter in this book, you will find "A Treasure and a Pearl." These precious jewels include lessons that have opened my eyes, given me hope and encouragement, and have lit my path to gaining and understanding a stronger relationship with God. I encourage you to find and write your own treasures and pearls. They are there within you and all around you to uncover and discover.

Long before I ever realized that I am a treasure and a pearl, an incident happened that changed the perception I had of my own worth. When I was in my senior year of college, my parents won a trip from the company where my dad worked. It would be a well-deserved vacation because my parents were caregivers for my grandmother who was living with them at the time. I could tell this situation was taking a toll on them. When they told us kids of their prize, I realized the trip would take place during my graduation ceremony. I had lived at home for the last several months while I was student teaching. I knew when I left college at Christmas time that I wouldn't be going back until graduation in May.

Living at home all of that time, I began to understand how difficult a task it was to care for someone with dementia. My grandmother could not remember whether she went to the bathroom, where she put her lit cigarette, or whether she ate a meal. My parents did not want to place her in a nursing home, but it became clear they could not care for her and keep her safe while they were at work. Even so, they worked hard as a couple to give her a happy, stable environment. I wasn't sure who would care for her while they were on their all expenses paid vacation, but I knew they needed the trip and should go.

My siblings also thought my parents needed to go on their vacation, so they asked me to forfeit my graduation ceremony because it would occur at the same time my parents would be gone on their trip. "Do I really need to participate in the ceremony to feel I have graduated?" I wondered. I would get my diploma either way and thought, "Well, maybe it isn't that big of a deal." My siblings were happy that I was willing to forego the ceremony so my mom and dad would get to go on their vacation after all. I decided that their trip to get some much-needed respite was more important than me "walking" at my college graduation, and when I told my mom that I had decided not to walk, and that she and my dad should have a great time on their trip, I remember her looking at me very perplexed. She said, "What trip?" I said, "You know, the one dad won." She told me that my father had already told his boss they would not be going on the trip because their daughter was graduating. She asked me why I thought they would be willing to miss my graduation, and she said to me, "Sue, don't you *know* how much we love you?" This was an epiphany for me because I realized just how much I was loved, but I also realized how bad I felt about myself. Somehow, I had thought my parents' vacation would take precedence over my college graduation!

IN RELATIONSHIPS

"In every encounter we either give life or we drain it;
there is no neutral exchange."

— Brennan Manning

If you are in a relationship with someone who sees you as anything less than beautiful, worthy, and a treasure and a pearl, know that it is not a reflection of your worth, but rather, a misconception on the part of the other person. People can be blinded by their own perceptions, and many people judge others based on their own opinions. Of course, we are all a work-in-progress, but nonetheless, no one except God is, or will ever be, perfect.

Do not allow others to define your worth. Instead, work on building an unshakable foundation with the one who loves *you* most of all: God. With His firm hand guiding you and helping you grow in the ways He sees fit, you cannot fail. Let no one else convince you that you are not valued or treasured. You are no less than a precious jewel.

You are indeed a blessing in the lives of those you touch, but you must believe and know this for yourself. Self-worth is an inside job and people learn how to treat you by the way you allow them to treat you and by observing the way you treat yourself. Treat yourself and others with love, kindness, and forgiveness because that is how you would want to be treated, and you will find that others will also begin to treat you in the same way. Ephesians 4:31-32 states, *"Let all bitterness, and wrath, and anger, and clamour, and evil speaking, be put away from you, with all malice: And be ye kind one to another, tenderhearted, forgiving one another, even as God for Christ's sake hath forgiven you."* In addition, Proverbs 16:24 says, *"Pleasant words are as a honeycomb, sweet to the soul, and health to the bones."* If you are someone who has been emotionally, physically, and/ or sexually abused, you may have difficulty determining what is "normal" in a relationship. Here is some great information to help you begin your healing process. Healthy relationships are based on:

- Caring
- Honesty
- Trust
- Mutual Respect
- Friendship
- Openness
- Mutual Pleasure
- Quiet Times
- Exciting Times
- Communication

Healthy relationships occur when those involved take personal responsibility for their own behavior and feelings. It is a fantasy to think someone other than God can "fix" you, complete you, or make you whole. While you can co-exist together with someone, support him or her, and build a quality and reciprocal life together, everyone is responsible for his or her own self-worth and joy. When two whole, complete, and joyful people come together, there is no limit to how wonderful that relationship can be!

In contrast, unhealthy relationships include behaviors that incite:

- Fear
- Jealousy
- Violence
- Manipulation
- Pain
- Intimidation
- Selfishness
- Mean Jokes
- Name Calling

Unhealthy relationships also include any kind of abuse. Abuse can be physical, emotional, sexual, verbal, spiritual, and through neglect. Here are some examples:

- Physical abuse is any type of violence: hitting, punching, pulling hair, kicking, or slapping.

- Emotional abuse can include bullying, teasing, humiliating, calling someone names, threatening, or betraying someone.

- Sexual abuse is forcing or coercing any type of sexual experience that is unwanted.

- Verbal abuse includes name calling, verbally demeaning or humiliating people in public or private, or abusive language directed at others.

- Spiritual abuse includes forcing spiritual beliefs on others or ridiculing and demeaning others' choices of spiritual practices, or using spiritual practices to manipulate or control other people.

- Neglect includes emotional and physical abandonment, not acknowledging others' wants or needs, and not including others in decisions that directly affect them.

All forms of abuse can create lifelong scars for those affected. If you or someone you know has been abused, you can reach out for help. You have a God-given right to be safe and treated with respect. No one has the right to abuse someone else.

Exercise:

Have you ever fallen prey to a relationship that included physical, emotional, or sexual abuse? What happened?

_____

_____

_____

_____

Have you believed that this abuse was what you deserved or were you too fearful to make a change? What messages were/are you saying to yourself?

_____

_____

_____

_____

Are you willing to make a change now? Whom can you reach out to for help?

_____

_____

_____

_____

If abusive relationships were part of your past, how did you get out, and how can you ensure you will not find yourself in the same situation again?

_____

_____

_____

_____

_____

_____

_____

_____

So what is normal in a relationship? Normal is determined by the people participating in the relationship. However, in general it would be safe to say that a healthy normal relationship includes love, respect, trust, honesty, and support. Also, understand that new relationships tend to be more passionate, and as a relationship matures, a natural shift occurs as each individual settles into the relationship and as the couple finds its natural rhythm. This shift does not mean that the relationship is dying, but rather that it is transforming into a deeper and possibly even more meaningful partnership and connection.

You are the only one who can determine whether or not you are in a healthy relationship. Sometimes it can be easier to turn a blind eye in a relationship because we want to see the best in someone. However, be sure and pay attention to any red flags that may appear because they could be indicators that your partner may not have the skill-set needed to have a healthy relationship or may even have abusive tendencies.

Exercise:

Which of the current relationships in your life are healthy?

_____

_____

_____

_____

Are you involved in any relationships that are unhealthy? How so?

_____

_____

_____

_____

Why do you suppose you have participated in these unhealthy relationships?

_____

_____

_____

_____

What would a healthy relationship look like to you with family, friends, children, and your mate?

_____

_____

_____

_____

_____

_____

_____

What commitment are you willing to make to yourself to be the healthiest you can be in your relationships with others? What healthy relationship skills do you need to develop and practice?

_____ _____

_____

_____

_____

_____

_____

_____

_____

Relationships are a two-way street, so we must be willing continually to hone our own healthy relationship skills.

IN THE WORKPLACE

> *"Difficulties are meant to rouse, not discourage.*
> *The human spirit is to grow strong by conflict."*
>
> **— William Ellery Channing**

Most businesses have a hierarchy of command, each with its own set of responsibilities; for example, administration or upper management, middle management, and front line staff. Just about everyone has someone to report to in a typical modern-day workplace, but that does not mean that any person is more valuable than any other person. Each individual has his or her own unique gifts and talents to share. Everyone has his or her own lessons to learn and to teach in this school of life. Even when lessons learned are negative, they are still lessons.

If you have conflict or difficulty at work, do your best to take personal responsibility for your part in the conflict and difficulty, and clean away your side of the street. It is your responsibility to own your behavior and to be aware of ways you can grow and develop personally. Also, keep in mind that you are not your job, and no matter what is happening at your job, you are still and always will be a treasure and a pearl. Let no external condition, circumstance, or challenge take this awareness from you.

SEEK TO UNDERSTAND

"O Divine Master, Grant that I may not so much seek,
To be consoled, as to console;
To be understood, as to understand."

— Saint Francis of Assisi

When Frank and I began dating, he often asked me, "How do you feel about that?" when we were discussing ordinary, everyday things. I had spent so many years in my first marriage allowing my opinions and feelings to be discounted that I had no practice at actually sharing and expressing them. When Frank asked me this question, I would become angry and feel forced to talk about my opinions and feelings. I felt angry because even I didn't quite understand my feelings and opinions, and quite frankly, it was shocking to me that someone actually wanted to know about them! I had no prior experience being "understood," and I had felt so misunderstood so much of the time.

What I learned from this experience was that I had many opinions and feelings, and after finally speaking my truth and being heard, I had developed a huge capacity for compassion for others. I *wanted* to know where other people were coming from. I *wanted* to learn how others were feeling.

Exercise:

Are you aware of your own feelings? Have you given up your right to have an opinion? Take a few moments to identify what you are feeling right now and answer these questions:

How are you feeling in your body right now?

_____

_____

_____

_____

Are you in touch with your own feelings? How are you feeling emotionally right now?

_____

_____

_____

_____

Do you consider your opinions and feelings to be important? As important as the opinions and feelings of others? Why or why not?

_____

_____

_____

_____

How can you make your feelings and opinions a priority in your life?

_____

_____

_____

_____

_____

To know it was okay to express my feelings was a liberating experience. For the first time in my life, my opinions and feelings became important. It was also important that I begin to understand those around me. My daughters and I made an agreement to begin working on our communication skills. Then one day when my daughter Jessie was about sixteen years old, she and her friends wanted to ride inner tubes down the river. Living near the river is a beautiful experience, but the river can also be dangerous. The day before this request, a serious accident in the river had occurred that involved the death of a teenager.

As a mom, I was so sad over this tragedy and could not imagine how the parents were coping with mourning the loss of their teenager's young life. The last thing I wanted to imagine or think about was my daughter hanging out on the river. What if something happened to her or one of her friends?

This sad event spurred me to tell Jessie she could not go. Of course, she wanted to know why I said, "No" since I usually would have said, "Yes." I explained to her that with the river incident so fresh in my mind and heart, I really just wanted not to worry about her that day. I explained it had nothing to do with her, but that I was still processing the drowning and asked whether for the next few days she would find another activity to do and that she stay away from the river.

Since we had been trying to work on understanding how the other felt over the months prior, Jessie was willing to listen to my feedback, and she honored my decision to stay away from the river by finding something else to do. By talking to her openly and honestly, I helped her understand that sometimes parents make decisions that don't seem to make sense necessarily, and sharing my feelings with her helped her have compassion for me and an understanding of why I made the decision I did.

Exercise:

Do you take the time to find out where the people who are important to you are coming from? Give an example.

_____

_____

_____

_____

_____

When your decisions affect other people and they become upset, how do you respond?

_____

_____

_____

_____

_____

What can you do to seek to understand those you love even more?

What do you need to do to become a better listener?

THE CLOSET

When Frank and I were engaged, we had to decide whose house to live in. Frank had bought his house in the year 2000 for him and his wife to live in together. At the time, he did not have a wife, but he was hoping that one day he would, and when that day came, he would be ready. Interestingly enough, I had moved to North Bend in 2000 and purchased a home with Max at that time.

Fast forward to after my divorce. When Frank and I met, fell in love, and were engaged, I did not really care where we lived. I was much more interested in spending my life with Frank than I ever was about where we would eventually reside. Since he had bought his home to share with his future wife, and that was going to be me, I thought we should live there. So Frank and I put my house up for sale.

All of this occurred before the housing market crashed, but even so, my home would not sell despite my best efforts, and I was left to care for a home that would require much more maintenance than I could provide by myself. Fortunately, God had it all figured out because as Frank and I moved ahead with our marriage plans, my daughters and a couple of their friends expressed interest in staying in my home so it would not be empty and our dog could stay as well.

Frank and I began the task of figuring out where things would go and what furniture we wanted to share together when we were married. He was very open to sharing his space, and as the time drew nearer, he was so excited finally to have his partner in life, for life.

We worked together to decide how to combine our belongings and what property would stay at my home or go with my daughters when they became ready to move out on their own, but something interesting happened one day while we were going through this process.

One day when we entered into the bedroom at Frank's house, he opened his double sliding door closet and pointed out how full it was; he remarked that half of his clothing and miscellaneous items would have to go to give me the remaining half of the closet. Without either of us understanding quite why, I sat down on the bed and began crying. "Why are you crying?" asked Frank. He wondered whether his offer was not good enough. He exclaimed that if I needed more space, we would find more. It was in that moment that I realized I had never had half of a closet. I had only been given the leftover space not needed by my former husband. For twenty-four years in my prior marriage, I had settled for crumbs, not even recognizing that I was worthy of more. Why did this make me cry? Because I was so overwhelmed by the generosity of what Frank was offering me. That God would put someone in my life who would be so loving, kind, and giving, that God would slowly reveal to me how He intended for a husband to treat a wife, *this* was the love of Christ.

Frank was showing me *that* kind of love, Christ's love, and I was so thankful that I was finally beginning to understand how much God loves me. He sent me a man who would treat me like a treasure and a pearl, a man who considered me and my wants and needs before he thought of himself, a man who would put my needs above his, a man who cared enough to ask what I desired and how I felt.

I began to realize that the reason I did not know how I felt for all those years before was that, for so long, I was not able to share my feelings. Because my sexual abuse was such a secret growing up and I could not share openly about what was happening to me, I had learned how to go underground and stuff my painful feelings down deep. This survival skill was one I carried into my adult life.

Later, in my marriage to Max, my feelings were rarely a consideration, and when I did share them, I was ridiculed and discounted for expressing them. I was treated as if my feelings somehow caused pain and discomfort in the relationship and that I was wrong for having feelings at all. I continued to stuff my feelings deep down inside of me, and it was not until I realized how much God loves me that I was able to begin accepting love and acknowledging that I am worthy of love.

Exercise:

Have you ever had a moment when you realized just how much God loves you? What happened and how did you know?

_____

_____

_____

_____

_____

How did this change your perception of yourself and your relationship with God?

_____

_____

_____

_____

Who in your life has modeled God's love for you through his or her behavior toward you, and how did you respond to this love?

_____

_____

_____

_____

Have you used denial to protect yourself from painful feelings in your life? Describe how.

_____

_____

_____

_____

The way Frank loves me unconditionally has opened up a metaphoric Pandora's Box in my heart. It has revealed the deep wounds that are still fresh and unhealed from my thirty-year relationship with someone who was completely emotionally unavailable and self-centered. The offering of half a closet was the catalyst for the surfacing of emotions that came from deep within my very soul. I thank the Lord for half a closet. It helped me gain valuable perspective about how distorted my thoughts were and how I allowed others to treat, or rather, mistreat me. Half a closet helped me identify how much denial I had in relation to my feelings and how I used this denial to protect myself from the painful reality of my own life. Half a closet has become a beautiful metaphor to describe my finding of my own voice and the importance of me speaking my truth and sharing and expressing my needs and feelings.

Over time, the Lord has taught me many things and continues to teach me. God reveals and heals my distorted thinking about myself and my relationships. In the deepest recesses of my heart and soul, where I have experienced the most pain, I want to be healed. I want to be healthy in my mind, body, and soul so I can better love Frank, all my family, and my friends. I also want to share my love and healing with you! To find out more about my work as a hope consultant, please visit my website at www.HopeAllowed.com.

RECONCILIATION TAKES TWO

*"It takes two to make a marriage a success and
only one to make it a failure."*

— Herbert Samuel

When Max and I were trying to hold our marriage together, we went to see a professional counselor in an attempt to heal the wounds we had incurred in our marriage. We saw the counselor for individual sessions on our own and for couple's sessions together.

I was in an individual session one afternoon when the counselor remarked that my husband was only 35 percent invested in the relationship. My dilemma was a big one; how could I, knowing that Max's heart was no longer in the marriage, continue to remain in the marriage and be a good wife? After all I had endured, including the emotional abuse and repeated infidelity, it was finally crystal-clear that if I were the only one invested in the relationship, it was not going to work. If two people are not invested in reconciliation, the invested person is powerless and the relationship is not going to heal. A great quote that clearly spells out this idea is:

"Relationships have peaks and valleys. To make a relationship last both people must be committed to the climbs, just as much as they are to admiring the grand views."

— Kaliana Dietrich

The reason why this information was such a hard chunk for me to swallow was because I did not believe in divorce or nullifying of the vow I had taken with my husband and the church. Some women of faith believe that because of their vows, they are to tolerate behavior that puts their own emotional, physical, and mental wellbeing in significant danger. They believe that if they choose to leave their marriages, they are sinning and they are filled with guilt and shame as a result. They believe they are failures, inadequate as women and wives.

Generally, a woman tends to feel responsible for her marriage's success or failure, but it takes two partners invested in a positive outcome with total commitment to make a marriage work. "If I were just a better _____ (wife, partner, lover), then maybe things could have worked out," I thought.

While I do not claim to have the answers to difficult moral and religious dilemmas, such as whether or not you should leave your marriage, or other tough life questions, I do know that God loves me and God loves you, too, and He does not stop loving us because a divorce happens. We live in a fallen and sinful world, and we all make mistakes. God is loving and forgiving to those who come to Him with a heart that desires His will, His mercy, and His truth. For myself, I cannot believe that He would want me to remain in a loveless and abusive marriage.

You see, mercy and truth are very different from each other. When we are coming from a background of abuse and oppression, we believe that abuse and oppression are what we deserve, but this is *not* the truth! As we continue to learn *God's* truth for ourselves, we know that He also has mercy and that we are in a constant state of learning, which means there will be times when we make mistakes, feel confused, and may not know what to do.

My truth while I was still married to my former husband was that I was never going to leave my husband and that I would always forgive him and work toward reconciliation. However, then I realized I was powerless over whether my husband was going to leave me.

I had not factored in the consideration that he might be unwilling to work toward reconciliation. I also realized I could never again trust my former husband due to his repeated infidelity. How could I then reconcile with that idea?

In my pain and confusion, my primary goal was to ask God what His will was for me. He knew it was not my desire to seek a divorce and that I was not safe in my marriage. He also knew my desire to feel safe and treasured. What I found, after finally letting go of my marriage, was that God was there to protect me and He had been with me all along; I just had to trust Him. Sometimes the hardest decision is the best decision, and sometimes God's will for me does not always seem like the best idea at the time. Isaiah 55:8-9 says, *"For my thoughts are not your thoughts, neither are your ways my ways, saith the LORD. For as the heavens are higher than the earth, so are my ways higher than your ways, and my thoughts than your thoughts."* God always knows the best and highest way for me, even when it is difficult for me to accept it or when it may not seem like the best way at the time.

HOW THE DIVORCE STOLE CHRISTMAS

In late December 2007, after thirty years of being together, Max disclosed to me that he never really loved me and didn't want to be with me anymore and that it was time to talk to the kids and let them know he wanted a divorce and for what reasons. Of course, as you can imagine, this devastated all of us. He also decided that, regardless of the current circumstances, we would all still be together for Christmas and that it would be great.

That Christmas was the worst Christmas ever. I was numb and in shock and it would be a few months before Max moved out. My kids stayed away from home as much as possible, and they were both out of state in college at the time. I felt so alone, even though and probably especially because Max was still in our home with me. Although he began sleeping in the basement, it was so upsetting that he was still there.

A couple of days after Christmas that year, I woke up and had some weird things going on with my body. I had to be taken to the emergency room. As it turned out, I had vertigo and couldn't walk much without losing my balance. I was pretty much stuck at home and needed help for a few days. I believe the vertigo was stress-induced because of what I was going through. Trying so hard to process how on earth my new life would transpire must have taken a huge toll on my mind, body, and spirit.

During the time I was home with vertigo, my recurring thoughts were of how I had allowed my divorce to steal my Christmas joy. I was thinking about the Dr. Seuss story *How the Grinch Stole Christmas*. The Grinch thought it was all about the presents, the tree, the decorations, and the roast beast. Eventually, he realized Christmas was maybe a bit more. At the end of the story, the circle of people holding hands and singing proved to the Grinch that Christmas was not about things but rather about family and friends. When I celebrated Christmas after the divorce, we still had the "things" since they were not stolen, but we didn't have the family we all wanted. We had been robbed and deceived. Our idea of what our family was and the truth we had always believed about our family was not true at all.

I realized my joy doesn't come from my idea of what I thought our family was; instead, it comes from my relationship with God, and He is the one who brings me joy. I chose to steal Christmas back because I realized I didn't have to allow the divorce to steal it forever. Healing happens! My health eventually improved, and in turn, I was given the strength I needed to help my children heal and become healthier, too. I am a healthy example for my children, and as a result of my experiences, I have also been able to help others find comfort in their pain.

Merry Christmas! These are two words I say aloud every year and they mean something different now. My new life is merry! I found that, in reality, my divorce never really stole Christmas at all, though it did temporarily steal the "merry" part. I thank God for never leaving my side through all of the pain and for allowing me to know what it feels like to heal.

If reconciliation takes two but you are the only one wanting to reconcile, you must trust that God has a plan. You cannot make someone love you despite your best efforts. The definition of reconciliation is: To re-establish a close relationship between, or to settle or resolve. Reconciliation is not the same as forgiveness. While you may forgive someone for his or her behavior, you may also still choose to move on. Moving on is difficult, but it may sometimes be necessary, and once again, you are not alone.

If you do not already have a loving God in *your* life, you can reconcile your relationship with Him at any time you choose. He is always there waiting for you with open arms. If you need help finding your path, I am here to help you. I have lived in the darkness, but I am now living in the light, the healing light of God's love.

Exercise:

Is there a relationship you need to reconcile? How can you make an effort to do so?

_____

_____

_____

_____

Have you had an experience with someone who was unwilling to reconcile? How did this affect your relationship with that person and with God?

_____

_____

_____

_____

Were you able to let the relationship go and to forgive or ask for forgiveness? How did it go?

_____

_____

_____

_____

Have you experienced shame and guilt, or felt you can never be good enough, or felt you sinned because of difficult choices you had to make, e.g., divorce or separation. Describe your experience.

_____

_____

_____

_____

Can you now ask God to forgive you for your past mistakes as well as offer forgiveness to someone who has hurt you? How will you seek His will for you from this point forward?

_____

_____

_____

_____

Some things happen in this lifetime that are beyond your control. God does not love you any less when you have to make difficult choices. No one deserves to be emotionally or physically abused or to live his or her life in a loveless and abusive situation. Trust in God's mercy and forgiveness. Forgive others and move forward to seek His will for you. Forgiveness will set you free!

Maybe there is something I can do for you on your journey. In my work as a hope consultant, I can help you on your path. If you or someone you know has a group that would benefit from my message, I am available to speak at your event or transformational weekend. For more information, please visit my website www.HopeAllowed.com

FRIENDSHIPS ARE CRITICAL

"The worst solitude is to have no real friendships."

— Francis Bacon

Friendships are critical to emotional and mental health. Every human being needs interaction with other humans. Newborns who are not nurtured experience failure to thrive and may even die without physical human contact and love.

People experience relationships in different ways. While some people may be introverted in their personalities and prefer a small circle of close, intimate friendships, others may be extroverted and host a large circle of friends and acquaintances. While neither personality is wrong or better than the other, friendships are necessary in relating and connecting with others, and in supporting one another in times of need.

Because you cannot build meaningful friendships in one day, it is paramount to create a circle of support, regardless of whether you are an introvert or extrovert. Creating friendships can be a new experience for people who have been isolated and oppressed. Where can you find such support? Here are some great suggestions to consider when seeking a support network:

- Join a book club or other group where you can meet new people and discuss shared information.

- Find a group at your local church. Many churches have gender specific groups and are a great place to share personal stories, gain support, and learn about building meaningful friendships based on the Word of God.

- Check your local newspaper for upcoming social and community events and attend them.

- Participate in a community service club such as Soroptimist International, Rotary, or the Lions Club. Not only will you meet great people, but you will participate in community service projects that benefit those most in need.

When I was having health problems and was sent home to recover shortly after a serious surgery, I could not rely on getting any support or help from my husband Max. Had it not been for a close friend, I do not know what I would have done. In my darkest hour, I was able to call my friend at the last minute because Max had left town, despite my request that he stay. I was afraid and alone, but my amazing friend put a schedule of people together who assisted me on a revolving basis. People came with meals, helped with chores, and helped me recover from my illness. I was so grateful to have such good people in my life. Because it is not fair to overload any one person with such responsibility, it meant a lot to have friends who could step in and help where they could.

If you have the tendency to isolate, consider building a support network of friends. These friends will be there for you in good times but also in bad. If you consider your spouse your only friend, you are putting him or her in the position to be the only one there for you emotionally and physically. Your spouse will be solely responsible for your care should you have any health problems, which leaves him or her with an unfair disadvantage. No one person should have to take responsibility for you during difficult times.

If you are married and your spouse is your "one support person," consider building a friendship with someone of your same sex on the outside. Women understand women, and men understand men. You can gain valuable support from your spouse, but it is also helpful to find gender specific friendships outside of your marriage.

How have you felt in the past when you knew you were able to help someone who needed it? Doesn't it feel great to be able to help someone else? We will discuss more about reaching out for help in the next chapter.

Exercise:

What do you consider character attributes of a good friend?

_____

_____

_____

_____

Which of the above character attributes do you have to bring to the table to share with your friends?

_____

_____

_____

_____

_____

Do you consider yourself an introvert or extrovert when it comes to making friends and building support for yourself? Describe some of these qualities.

_____

_____

_____

_____

_____

Have you ever expected any one person to take on unfair responsibility for you? Who and how?

_____

_____

_____

_____

_____

Where can you go to build support, and whom can you lean on to help you when you need it most?

_____

_____

_____

_____

How can you be a support, and what do you have to offer your friends when they need you most?

_____

_____

_____

_____

SUMMARY

You are more valuable than you can ever know. You are indeed God's treasure and His pearl. You deserve the best in all your relationships. Build relationships based on mutual respect and trust. Treat yourself well and surround yourself with others who treat you well, too. Do your best to understand yourself, to understand others, and to understand God. The closer you become to your Maker, the more you will be able to trust your own decisions and feel His mercy.

You cannot make someone love you, and you do not deserve a life of suffering. Do what you can to forgive and to let go of people, places, and things that do not support your wellbeing. Instead, do your best to create friendships that are supportive, reciprocal, and positive.

Thus far in this book, you have learned about the value of not keeping secrets that hurt you, the advantages of being mindful and not speaking to others in anger, and how to combat the loneliness that seems to permeate the world today. You have also learned that you are more valuable than you have ever known, and by trying to understand others, you will better understand yourself.

We have discussed the ideas that reconciliation can be achieved only when both people choose to reconcile, we can reconcile with God in an effort to experience peace and forgiveness, and there is value in building crucial friendships, especially when we have been isolated and oppressed. In this book's remaining chapters, we will begin learning about and practicing hands-on tools for building hope in all areas of life. You can pick up, practice, and use these tools in any combination. Keep an open mind as you move forward and gain valuable insight into The Hope Factor.

A TREASURE AND A PEARL

What we *believe* will dictate our actions, and having trust is a huge part of believing, even though it can be difficult to trust sometimes. Maybe you have given your trust over to someone or to an organization that has let you down. Humans are fallible and we all disappoint someone sometimes. When I was seeking something to fill the void in my life, I decided to believe that the messages I was receiving about God were true. Proverbs 3:5-6 says: "*Trust in the LORD with all thine heart; and lean not unto thine own understanding. In all thy ways acknowledge him, and he shall direct thy paths.*" Believe that you are valuable and that relationships matter and can be healthy. When you begin to hear repeatedly what it is you need to hear in order to trust again, you will begin to believe the truth. I trusted the friend who invited me to church, and I saw something in her life that I wanted for my own. I decided to believe that what was being said at church and what my friend was also saying was true. So if it was true, then what?

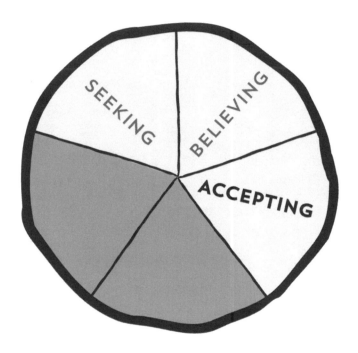

Accepting: To receive as valid or correct.

Chapter Three

HEALING AND HOPE

"Trying to suppress or eradicate symptoms on the physical level can be extremely important, but there's more to healing than that; dealing with psychological, emotional and spiritual issues involved in treating sickness is equally important."

— Marianne Williamson

HAVE AN ADVOCATE

An advocate is a person who argues for the cause of another person, and in the context of this book, an advocate is someone who can speak for you when you are unable to speak for yourself.

For instance, a friend of mine went to doctors' appointments with another friend who was diagnosed with breast cancer because she was very frightened, and rightly so. Because of her fear, she seemed to have some sort of information block, so my friend attended her doctor visits with her so she could listen, take notes, and later remind her of what had been discussed. My friend would write down important questions so they could get answers during the doctor visits. This situation is an example of an advocate.

In 2005, Max and I had planned a cruise to take place the following year, but we were unable to go because over the course of the year I began having some health issues that required a hysterectomy. The day of my hysterectomy, I was alone because Max had another priority. If it were not for my sister and the people from church, I would have literally gone through this experience by myself. While it was disappointing and hurtful to me that Max had little interest in my health or concern over my need for major surgery, I was so grateful and blessed to have people in my life who could be there for me.

Within days after getting home from the surgery, I knew I was not healing well and something was wrong, but after a check-up, I was told by my doctor that everything was okay. I returned to work six weeks after my surgery and began planning another trip with Max. Lo and behold, the day before the trip, I woke up in horrible pain. At the emergency room, I was informed that I would need emergency surgery for appendicitis. Max was angry that I needed emergency surgery because it meant he would have to miss an important work engagement.

Once I returned home after *this* surgery, my pain did not subside and I knew something was wrong. I was not able to eat or sleep, but five days later, at my follow-up appointment, my doctor once again told me that everything was fine. I did not have an advocate and the doctor just kept giving me more medication for the pain, but it was not alleviating the problem. In desperation, two weeks later I called a friend for help; she insisted I go to a different doctor and referred me to her own physician.

Within minutes of talking with her, the new doctor affirmed that something was wrong, and she sent me for a type of x-ray called a CT scan. The CT scan indicated that I had a hematoma and was bleeding internally. It would take weeks, maybe even months, for me to heal completely, and it was suggested by the new doctor that I quit my job and give my body time to heal.

After two successive surgeries, my body was spent. I knew I had to give myself the gift of time to heal in order to recover physically and emotionally. I did quit my job despite protests from Max. However, shortly after quitting my job, my massage therapist told me she felt a lump in my thyroid.

This time, I made an appointment to see what the lump was. When the time for the appointment came, I had family visiting from out of town. Max did not think he needed to go, so my mother-in-law volunteered to attend the doctor's appointment with me. At this point, I had learned the value of gaining support. As it turned out, I needed a biopsy fast! My mother-in-law and I looked at each other in the elevator after leaving the doctor's office and confirmed through our tears that we had both heard the same thing; the lump might be cancerous. I was so glad I had another set of ears with me to hear what was said.

My biopsy was scheduled for the following day. After a sleepless night, I realized that although I had already learned so much about asking people for help, it was now time to ask God for help. I decided and affirmed in my heart and soul that no matter the outcome, I would praise God. All of this must be happening for a reason, I thought. Whether or not the lump was cancerous, I would find a way to see it as a blessing. Max decided to take me to this appointment. On the way to get the biopsy, the song "Blessed Be Your Name" by Matt Redmond came on the radio. As the lyrics state, I believe God does give and take away, and I knew in that moment that I was going to bless His name regardless of the biopsy's outcome.

Shortly after the biopsy, the doctor came back into the private office and said, "Today is one of the days I am so happy to have my job and to tell you that you do not have cancer." God had lifted me up; He had carried me through and given me the peace I needed to trust in Him. As it turned out, the lump later grew back, and eventually, I had it removed from concern it could stick to my vocal chords and cause damage. However, all of these experiences where my very life hung in the balance gave me immense strength and trust in my God.

Not long after this event, I found out that Max had been living a double life our entire marriage. You would think at this point I would have cowered down and given up. But no, I did not! This crushing emotional blow was no match for my newfound spiritual condition. I knew that after everything I had been through, God would surely help me through this. I had built an unshakable and beautiful relationship with my Creator and no person, circumstance, or condition could take away my strength and the growth I had experienced while learning to trust and rely on Him. Through prayer, I asked God what to do and was led to give Max water and food. God told me that the one thing I could do, and the right thing to do, was to have compassion and provide meals and drink for Max, despite our circumstances. In this way, I could still serve and be true to myself by following God's lead.

During this same time, I was told I had a grapefruit sized tumor in my abdomen. Although my doctor believed it probably was not cancerous, he decided it would need to be removed. Two weeks before the Thanksgiving holiday, I had the surgery to remove the tumor. This was the fourth surgery within two years and Max was not around to help. Once again, I was so fortunate to have a loving group of people who came and assisted me around the clock once I was discharged home. There was no way I would have been able to take care of myself, and I was so blessed to be surrounded by friends. I was finally at a place in my life where I could accept the help that was so graciously offered.

I had hope for the first time in my life. From the top of my head to the tips of my toes, I had hope and no person or worldly condition was a worthy opponent for the fight I was fighting now! Not only had I learned the lesson that I could and would ask for help and seek an advocate when I needed it most, but I had become my own advocate in the process. This was truly a big step for me.

When you are on your knees, get an advocate. When you feel you are all alone, reach out and ask someone to accompany you. You should never have to face your fear alone. There are those who love you, will be there for you, and will show you and teach you how to love yourself when you feel you are at your very bottom. There are those who will carry you through if you but ask, and you have a strong and mighty God working on your behalf.

Exercise:

Who are your advocates, those people you can count on to speak for you if you are unable to speak for yourself?

_____

_____

_____

_____

Have you ever been an advocate for someone else who was unable to speak for him- or herself? Who and when?

_____

_____

_____

_____

How did you feel about yourself when you were able to assist someone else who needed you?

_____

_____

_____

_____

Do you insist on "going it" alone even though you know you need help? Can you see the value to others when you allow them to help you? Explain.

_____

_____

_____

_____

Being there for someone else can help that person heal emotionally, physically, and spiritually. Allowing someone else to help you when you need it most is also healing.

ASKING FOR HELP

"Part of the healing process is sharing with other people who care."

— **Jerry Cantrell**

Asking for help can be hard. Some people are better at giving and others are better at receiving, but if you do not learn to receive or cannot receive because you have too much pride or arrogance, you will be the one who misses out. It is okay to ask for help! Get to the place where you can receive help; get to the place where you can own your blessings. Accept help when it comes your way, and pass it on to others when they need help too. Here are some questions to ask yourself when you are struggling with receiving help from others:

- Are you being self-serving?
- Are you not receiving because you truly believe you should not accept it?
- If your heart is pure in the motives of your actions, why would it not be okay for you to receive?
- Do you believe you are worthy of receiving?

Exercise:

Knowing when and how to give can be confusing at times. Consider these questions when you are not sure about giving or how to help:

What do you have to give? Time? Money? Moral support?

_____

_____

_____

_____

_____

Are you *always* supposed to help others if you have the means to do so? Give an example.

_____

_____

_____

_____

_____

What are your values and morals about giving?

_____

_____

_____

_____

_____

How do you discern whether or not to give?

_____

_____

_____

_____

_____

Is there someone in your life who needs your help right now? How can you help him or her?

_____

_____

_____

_____

If you are unsure whether giving is the right thing to do, try trusting your gut, following your heart, and being obedient to what you believe God wants for you and for the other person. Listen to your inner voice and you will begin to understand what you are being led to do. When in doubt, pray about it and be patient until the right answer comes to you.

ASKING GOD FOR HELP

The week of Thanksgiving, my girls, Max, and I were scheduled to fly to the Midwest to spend the holiday with my family, but Max did not show up, so my daughters and I took the trip alone. For six days, I struggled to process everything in my heart. It became very clear at this point that something was gravely wrong with Max.

The day after Thanksgiving, with a house full of people, I went into the closed garage where we were staying and got into the car. I cried out to God with all my heart and soul. Somehow, all this time, I had thought I had some control over the outcome of my marriage. I believed that if I just worked hard enough and did all the right things, Max and I would be able to hang in there and work it out. For the first time, it became clear that my marriage was out of my hands and that the outcome would have to be God's decision. I turned my marriage over to God with all my heart that day, and in December, Max asked for a divorce. Jeremiah 33:3 states, "*Call unto me, and I will answer thee, and shew thee great and mighty things, which thou knowest not.*"

When I was calling out in pain because I did not know how to love any less, when I was on my knees broken, I found a faith that gave me the confidence to know that God would show me great and mighty things. I would then be able one day to tell others just how great and mighty God is. During my darkest times when I asked for help, I was not always given the answers right away. Rather I was humbled to know that He did hear me and that He would answer in His time.

Asking God for help was not an easy thing for me, but I had a personal relationship with Jesus already, so I knew I could accomplish things in His strength if I could determine what it was He wanted me to do. It was only then that I was able to hear and receive the message of God and that was when He told me to love Max by giving him drink when he was thirsty and food when he was hungry, and I thought to myself, "I think I can do that." I was praying God would bring Max to a place of reconciliation with Himself and with me.

The song lyrics to "Kindness" by Chris Tomlin, which I had learned in church, kept coming into my head. The song talks about the kindness of God that leads us to repentance. One evening at dinner when I was feeding and giving Max drink, he asked, "Why are you being so kind to me?" This moment was exciting to me because I was actually able to show Max the love of God by being obedient to

His request. I had loved Max the way God asked me to love him and Max was able to see God's kindness through my actions. That was confirmation for me that I was doing what God wanted me to do, and *in that* there was comfort, and *that* was a great and mighty thing.

While my efforts did not bring Max to repentance as I had originally hoped, they still brought me closer to my God because I knew it was really my relationship with God that mattered and that pleasing Him was the most important thing. By asking for help, I was able to get through that difficult time and begin the process of forgiveness. Take a few moments in this next exercise to reflect on the concept that regardless of the choices, behaviors, and responses of others, you can still make choices that are loving and kind.

Exercise:

Have you ever loved someone who made bad and/or selfish choices that affected you at your core? What happened?

_____

_____

_____

_____

Have you been able to forgive others for their choices? What was your process?

_____

_____

_____

_____

What happens to you when you remain resentful and angry with someone else for his or her behavior? Who pays the price physically and emotionally for your resentment and anger?

_____

_____

_____

_____

What would be the benefits to you now to turn this resentment and anger over to God and to ask for a solution to your problem?

_____

_____

_____

_____

What would be the kind and loving way to respond to someone who has hurt you? What can you do to take the high road, the loving road, so you can experience peace in your heart and do God's will?

_____

_____

_____

_____

THE COMMUNITY AND HOPE

Do you know where you can go in your community to get help when needed? In the next section, I will share with you some of the amazing and noteworthy programs and helpers in my own community that are there to help those in need and provide advocacy, food, shelter, and important services. But most importantly, they provide hope. They are modeling God's kindness and love each and every day. You may already have similar programs in your community, but if you do not, my intention is to share these great places with you so you may be able to take these ideas and help people in your own town.

Valley Renewal Center

Sometimes it takes a whole village to come together in the spirit of love to help those most in need. The Valley Renewal Center has done exactly that. Near the end of 2012, the police chief in my community held a public meeting to try to find ways to address the issue of homelessness. Twenty-nine people attended, including elected officials, and it was clear that fear was a driving element of the meeting. The police chief classified the homeless in four different categories: the chronically homeless, the homeless who live in their vehicles, the couch surfers, and the newly homeless due to domestic violence issues.

For people who fit into the category of owning a vehicle, the city was forced to tow cars that were parked illegally, which created a moral dilemma. How do you, in good conscience, tow a vehicle, knowing you are taking away someone's only housing and possessions?

Another issue was the many homeless teens who had finished high school but then had nowhere to go. For many of these homeless teens, the only mentors and support they experienced had been while in school. Once high school was completed, they were on their own with no clear direction or support.

After a few initial meetings, an advisory council was formed that consisted of those who were interested in helping the homeless. Community concerns brewed in the background, and an undertow of fear came from many. One of these concerns included: If we open a shelter, will it bring even more homeless people to our community?

The advisory council worked very hard to address these concerns by developing an action plan and securing initial funding to open a "winter shelter" as a starting point. The goal was to open before the end of the year but there was still much to do. Sleeping mats, blankets, and of course, more money were needed to facilitate even the basic needs of those who would be staying in the shelter.

A local non-profit organization, Congregations for the Homeless, which specializes in the running of homeless shelters, partnered with the team to help get the program up and running. Its members attended the local meetings to address questions, calm fears, and guide our community toward the opening of a safe, successful shelter. Congregations for the Homeless agreed to manage the shelter because it recognized that its many years of experience would be crucial for the winter shelter's success.

As it turned out, despite ongoing concern, everything necessary to run the shelter successfully was provided, including sleeping mats, blankets, supplies, food, and money for paid and volunteer staff, as well as staff training. Two local churches agreed to provide the facility and the Snoqualmie Valley Winter Shelter opened on December 23rd! As soon as the doors opened, the meal volunteer calendar on the Internet filled up completely. People from local community organizations, the school across the street, local churches, and private citizens were bringing in breakfast and dinner every day for the guests. The outpouring of love and support was overwhelming! God is good and there is nothing a community cannot do when people pull together for a common purpose!

Miracles happen when the heart and the mind come together in a group of like-minded, passionate, and compassionate people. These people were able to find creative solutions together and "get 'r done," so to speak! As a direct result of the Valley Renewal Center and the Snoqualmie Valley Winter Shelter, many people have reconnected with their families, and so many others have received the resources they needed so desperately to get back on their feet.

Lacey's Story

I have a wonderful friend named Lacey who gave me permission to share her story. After struggling with infertility, what happened in her life was nothing short of miraculous! Here is her story in her words:

> Infertility! The word still weighs heavy on my heart. The women before me pumped out kids like you would not believe. I felt defective. The thought of never having a biological child was devastating. It was not until I fully accepted this reality that my life would be changed forever.
>
> After several failed attempts, there was only one option left for my husband Rob and me to conceive and that option came with many unknowns. Rob and I sat across from the doctor as she explained what felt like a never-ending list of risks. One of our biggest concerns was a multiple pregnancy. Rob shared that he could handle twins, but having triplets terrified him.

The doctor looked us in the eyes, put her hands on the table between us, and said, "That will never happen to you. Lacey will be lucky to have one." The doctor could not have been more wrong. A couple of months later, I was pregnant with quadruplets!

It was suggested by the doctor that I have a procedure referred to as "selective reduction." How could I possibly choose two fetuses to abort after trying for this pregnancy so long? I would risk everything, my health and the babies, to do what I believed in. The question remained, "How were we going to get through this?" We felt inadequate to care for four premature babies, and let me mention also that we had three stepchildren. Seven children? How would we do this?

First, I had to make it through bedrest. This was something I had not prepared for. After two and a half months of living at the hospital away from my family, I felt isolated and beyond lonely. Then something happened I did not expect...visitors! People I hardly knew and some I had never met before. Mostly, they were from our church and some from the community. I had thought my extended family would be my only strength, but now I sought comfort in new relationships as well. I believed God was recruiting them for the journey that was quickly approaching, a journey He knew we could not embark on alone.

While I was hospitalized, our church filled the freezer at home with meals for Rob and the kids. In addition, a team of over fifty volunteers was formed and led by a woman named Cece. She was an acquaintance then, but she soon earned the title of "my angel." There were even teams within the team, and a couple of reliable gals made themselves T-shirts. The team would be ready to help care for the babies when they came home. About two months after birth, our four perfect, tiny miracles did come home one at a time.

When that time came, it was difficult for me to accept the help. My instinct, however unrealistic, was to care for my babies solo. I had to open my home and receive the blessings from those in my church and community. Initially, they came in flocks. There were two volunteers in the morning and two for the afternoon, five days a week. They gave me the gift of sleep so I could make it through those long nights. One volunteer named Kimberly came alongside us and really made our family her local ministry. She is still along for the ride today. It has been six years and "Auntie Kimmy" has never wavered in her support. The friendships this experience has brought are like no other.

I know now why all those people were brought into our lives. I was able to let go of the guilt of needing help and truly embrace the gift of their time and compassion for our family. I was even able to learn how to ask for what I need and then accept it when it came. Each person who walked through our door offered us hope that we could get through those first few years, and I am forever grateful. Psalm 71:14 states: "*But I will hope continually, and will yet praise thee more and more.*"

Lacey's story is a great example of how God provides for us sometimes even when we do not realize the kind of help we need. When we are able to reach out and allow others to come into our lives to help us, we invariably get our needs met and give others the gift of knowing they were able to make a difference for someone else.

The North Bend Theatre

The North Bend Theatre has been in our community for more than seventy years, and the owners have made it a point to allow the community to use its space for community fundraising and other events. For generations, the North Bend Theatre has served as a community-meeting place for families and friends of all ages.

When the theatre needed to update its equipment and could not afford to do so on its own, the owners reached out to the community they had faithfully served for so many years. Their request for funds would make it possible for them to purchase a new digital projector, which would carry the theatre over another great seventy years so they could continue showing movies, operas, concerts, and other special events. They would have to close their doors if they were unable to convert to the digital projector because the movie distributors no longer offered 35-millimeter films. Additionally, with a digital projector, the North Bend Theatre would be able to provide the latest 3-D movies, but it would cost nearly $100,000!

A mail appeal for help was sent out to the community by the theatre owners. In it were some very clever fundraising ideas. Community members could purchase a "Hollywood Boulevard" style star in the sidewalk outside the theatre and see their names engraved on large brass stars in the theatre lobby. They would also have chairs with their names on them to recognize them for their support. Another option was to buy a date with the theatre owners to a Seattle film screening and lunch. Contributions ranged from $50 to $5,000.

What happened next was nothing short of a miracle! This subsequent letter from the North Bend Theatre to the community members says it all:

Dear Friends of the North Bend Theatre,

On May 1st, we embarked on an effort to raise $100,000 for a new digital projector. Today, just four months later, as a community we have raised nearly $98,000! This paves the way for the future of our theatre, ensuring that we will make the conversion to digital projection!

More than 550 amazing families and businesses have donated to our fundraiser! One-third of the money raised has come from contributions of $100 or less, one-third from contributions between $100 and $500 and one-third from $1,000 and $2,500. This has truly been a community-wide project! It has been so heartwarming to read such encouraging comments on our website and rewarding to see how treasured our theatre is in the community. Thank you, thank you, and thank you again for the generous support!

Congratulations to this terrific community for ensuring that the North Bend Theatre will continue to be an active part of the Snoqualmie Valley for years to come! We so appreciate your support, patience, and confidence, and we thank you from the bottom of our hearts.

Sincerely, Jim and Cindy Walker

Tuesday, September 10, only four months after the theatre's mail appeal, Jim and Cindy Walker were able to install their new projector. This kind of heartfelt progress is what happens when a community and its people reach out and share their resources. For so many years, the owners of the North Bend Theatre have given so much, and now they will be able to continue giving thanks to the support of those in the community.

Snoqualmie Valley YMCA

The Snoqualmie Valley YMCA provides great services to my local community, especially for children. Below is a description of its wonderful overnight camping program, as told by a local YMCA board member:

> For more than 100 years, the YMCA's overnight camping program has inspired kids to pursue their potential while discovering more about who they are, what they can do, and how to share their gifts to strengthen community. These experiences give kids increased confidence, new knowledge, and a sense of adventure, while making them realize they can make a positive impact at school and in the community with lessons learned.
>
> The community has recognized the importance of giving kids the camp experience. They have seen the benefit of what a week of camp can do to transform the attitudes and direction of our young people. They have seen at an early age how important positive adult role modeling is and the impact this modeling has on our kids. Our community knows we are providing the opportunity to shape today's youth into tomorrow's community leaders.

Each summer, fifty kids in our community who need this type of experience, but do not have the means to provide it, are given the chance to board a bus and simply "go to camp" due to the amazing donors in our valley. What they receive is far more than just a chance to go to camp. The memories the children gain will extend far beyond their youth, and they experience a rare opportunity they otherwise would not have experienced due to being unable to afford it. The community members who donate money for this event find great satisfaction because they know what an important and inspirational experience they have created for children!

Rancho Laguna's HEART

Rancho Laguna's HEART program is another amazing and inspirational organization. It assists forgotten, neglected, and abused animals. HEART (Home of Equine Assisted Rescue Therapy) nurses these animals back to health with love and compassion, and it helps them eventually find forever homes.

Tina Laguna is the founder of HEART. She left her corporate career to meet a need in her community to rescue and safely place abused horses and other animals in "forever homes."

Conversely, Tina's rescue pets provide therapy for people who have been through abuse or other kinds of traumatic experiences. HEART is a place where therapists come to provide healing and therapy in a nurturing and safe environment to those who need it most. The community helps with donations and volunteers help with maintaining the property and caring for the animals. Below is one story Tina agreed to share with me:

> One heartwarming story we can share involves a very cold, icy February morning when HEART received a call from Animal Control regarding two horses needing rescue. While HEART had no space left to rescue the horses, after finding out there was nowhere else for the horses to go, the woodshed was emptied to make room for them.
>
> The two mares, mom and daughter, Rose age twenty-five and Ruby age ten, were two of five surviving horses. Nine other horses and many other farm animals had died on the same farm due to starvation and neglect. Later that night, Ruby and Rose were loaded into the trailer and traveled quietly to their new home, the woodshed, without a peep. In it, they would be warm, sheltered, and fed, and they could begin to heal from their neglect and abuse.
>
> Ruby and Rose were near starvation and very underweight and their care would be around the clock and labor intensive. They had no sparkle in their eyes and made no "nicker," the characteristic sound made by healthy horses.
>
> We prayed around the clock that they would find the will to live, and each morning when I went to check on their progress, I hoped to find them still alive. With each passing day, they got healthier, and then after about a month, one night I went out for their last feeding of the evening, and hope of hopes, I found they were both lying down, comfortably resting, and

they greeted me with the sweetest midnight "nicker" I could have ever hoped to hear.

Six months later, with recovery under their belts, it was time to find out whether these horses were just pets or riding horses. I had spent time brushing them every day, which they loved; now it was time for the saddles. As it turned out, they were well-seasoned and had wonderful manners.

During the spring and summer of the two mares' recovery, one very special little girl named Gia bonded with Ruby. Having spent nearly every day at Rancho Laguna helping take care of and learning to ride Ruby, she and her family decided they wanted to be Ruby's forever home, and on that last day of summer, the hope of a little girl and the hope of a horse collided. To this very day, Gia and Ruby are still spending time together, loving, laughing, and hoping together.

Rose is now almost thirty-one and still living here at Rancho Laguna's HEART. She is a huge contributor and member of our equine therapists and provides hippo (physical) therapy and PTSD (Post-Traumatic Stress Disorder) therapy. The prayers I said under my breath on behalf of Rose and Ruby were answered in spades!

Rancho Laguna's HEART program is a great example of hope and how one woman's dream has helped so many, humans and animals alike.

In the Field Ministries

John and Kimberly Calhoun felt compelled to start a ministry in the community of Nabisooto, Uganda, where funds were desperately needed to provide water, schools, and basic needs for those living in their village. In order to provide those basic needs, John and Kimberly reached out to their own community here at home in the Snoqualmie Valley. They also had something else to offer the community of Nabisooto, which was prayer. One such story, told here by John and Kimberly, encapsulates the hope that In the Field Ministries (ITFM) has given the community of Nabisooto, Uganda:

Eight-year-old Rosemary stares up at the mud walls of her small home listening to the chickens peck at the ground in the next room. Her mother, grandmother, and two baby sisters sleep beside her on old grass mats because they do not have a mattress. Rosemary swats away the mosquitoes, hoping none of them carry malaria. Her future is bleak and her duty is to stay at home and care for her sisters because school is too far away and expensive to attend. Rosemary's mother is ill and she has to stay near home in case her mother collapses and needs help.

Nabisooto has no running water or electricity. Rosemary will get water from the swamp and carry the heavy jugs all the way home. She will always feel dirty and wear dirty clothes and her lungs will remain congested from breathing in the dirt from her mud home all day and night. She will get malaria often, as will her other family members, and the odds are that she or one of her siblings will not survive it at some point.

If Rosemary does survive, she will more than likely have children of her own at a very young age and will move to another mud hut. Life will be hard, and she will work in the fields all day and collect firewood for cooking. She will wash clothes and clean her children in a small plastic tub, day in and day out, the same day full of hard work awaiting her.

When ITFM arrived in Nabisooto right across the street from Rosemary, they put in a deep-water well, so now Rosemary just has to cross the road to fill her jugs with clean water. ITFM also built a clinic, and now medicine is readily available for Rosemary and her family if they get sick. A school was built, and Rosemary is allowed to attend with her sister because it is so close to her home. Rosemary's future has changed. She studies about disease prevention in school and takes this knowledge home so now her family will get sick less often. She does well in school and plans for a career so she can help her family. Rosemary has hope now. She has a spring in her step, she looks different, and she talks differently. Hope has changed who she is.

Not only does In the Field Ministries provide hope in Nabisooto, Uganda, but its ministry has also touched six other villages. ITFM is making a huge impact by inspiring individuals and communities in Uganda and right here at home.

Boxley Music Fund

Not often do you hear about a restaurant offering hope to students and musicians alike. At Boxley's in North Bend, Washington, you will find a special place for the whole family to experience delicious food and to get their souls soothed by wonderful music at the same time. Boxley's has a music fund, and one of the board members of the fund has agreed to share a little bit about it here:

Danny and Robyn Kolke's desire was to provide a place where people could enjoy jazz music and eat for a price most people could afford. Elite musicians often visit Boxley's to play music and encourage young musicians to continue learning about their own musical skills and talents.

The Kolkes also started a non-profit organization, the Boxley Music Fund. The purpose of the music fund is to promote live jazz programs for performance and education. To accomplish this, the music fund accepts donations from the community and customers. Audiences from all over western Washington come to Boxley's to enjoy music performed by students and professionals alike. In addition, Boxley's restaurant is now owned by the Boxley Music Fund, making this a truly unique community-supported venue and program.

This ingenious model is changing lives in our community! The music fund exposes students to live performances of jazz, and it provides clinics and teaching forums with professional artists, performance opportunities with professionals, and scholarship programs to help support private lessons. The funds also create recording opportunities, assistance with creating demo recordings, and access to professional musicians in a family-friendly environment, and the musicians then participate in a regional jazz festival.

On specific nights of the week, there are vocal workshops, special clinics, private lessons, and mentorship and performance opportunities for students to perform on the same stage as professionals. These are inspiring and creative ways for young musicians to learn and grow in their skills and love of jazz.

People can donate to the non-profit music fund in several ways, and the ripple effect in our community is immeasurable. For example, one family has a child who has a love and gift for music but no funds to attend music lessons. Another example is the child who needs music to promote his actual wellbeing, and while that might sound like an exaggeration, many people turn to music to decrease their stress, reduce depression, to help reframe negative thoughts into positive ones, and simply to gain hope. Music builds confidence and is literally therapeutic.

Musicians commonly need to work jobs that do not involve their music in order to meet their basic needs. Boxley's offers them the opportunity to play the music that feeds their souls. It makes them very happy and they get to give back and help other young musicians, which is very gratifying.

Billy Joel said it very well when he said, *"I think music in itself is healing. It's an explosive expression of humanity. It's something we are all touched by. No matter what culture we're from, everyone loves music."*

Share Your Story

All of the above amazing stories are accounts from everyday people, organizations, and service providers doing extraordinary things. My hope is that by reading them, you will see just how valuable you are to your own community. Do not allow your fear of connecting with community agencies like these keep you from asking for help if you need it or from allowing you to give back to your community. We all have something to give whether it is talent, time, expertise, or even money.

Just as it takes a whole village to raise a child, it takes a whole community to provide hope to someone who has experienced trauma and adversity. When we become willing to share our own stories, we give others hope, and we give them permission to do the same. It has been so important for me to share my story in this book and through my personal encounters. I know my story has and will continue to help many people. Someone needs to hear your story too. What is it you have to share that may help someone else? What hope can you offer to another?

Do not let your fear of the unknown or feelings of inadequacy keep you from sharing your God-given talents with others. If you have time, expertise, money, or most importantly, hope, then share it freely. What you give will return to you in droves.

But let us go back to the word *fear* for just a moment. In the next section, we will talk about fear specifically and how not to let it cripple or limit you. You will also gain some valuable tools and strategies to overcome it. The big question is: Do you have fear, or does fear have you?

When we begin to have faith and to reach out to our community, we find a host of support from people and organizations. There is so much to learn about what is going on in our very own communities. You do not have to go through hard times alone and there is help available. Do not allow your fear to stifle your growth and keep you from reaching out to others. Did you know that fear is the opposite of faith? In the next section, we will examine fear and why it is so important to begin facing and letting go of it.

FEAR

Here are some great quotes that drive home the idea that we must let go of fear. We can have faith and use God's strength when we feel we do not have enough of our own to carry us through:

"Yea, though I walk through the valley of the shadow of death, I will fear no evil: for thou art with me; thy rod and thy staff they comfort me."

— Psalm 23:4

"The fear of man bringeth a snare: but whoso putteth his trust in the LORD shall be safe."

— Proverbs 29:25

Fear is the four-letter word that can paralyze, cripple, or limit you from having, being, or doing what you truly want to do in your life! Fear is the number one offender that prevents you from healing your old wounds that continue to haunt you and stunt your growth. While everyone experiences feelings of fear (and it is important to note that fear is, indeed, just a feeling), dwelling on fear or letting fear take over can be counter-productive, create feelings of depression and low self-worth, and actually affect your decision-making process.

I have heard many acronyms for fear over the years, including:

Face Everything And Recover

and

False Evidence Appearing Real

Fear *really* comes from being afraid that we will lose something we already have, or that we will not gain something we want. Fear can be based in selfishness and self-centeredness when we allow our instincts to take over. Here is a great quote from Scripture that supports the idea that you are meant to grow and shine brightly and to share your gifts with the world:

"For God hath not given us the spirit of fear; but of power,
and of love, and of a sound mind."

— 2 Timothy 1:7

Fear can make us feel inadequate and can steal our happiness. Here are some common fears that, if left unchecked, can begin to affect our self-worth and peace of mind:

- Fear of failure: The fear of failure can be scary. Taking action involves taking risks, and taking risks can feel frightening and uncomfortable.

- Fear of not having enough food, money, sex, attention, and so on.

- Fear that you won't be able to handle your feelings when you begin to face whatever issues you have avoided.

These can be stubborn and persistent fears, especially for those who have experienced trauma, poverty, or abuse. Many other fears can limit your ability to heal and hinder your personal development. Some examples include speaking in public, heights, mice, and spiders.

Fear affects us from the inside out. It can lead to anxiety, take charge of our decision-making process, and cause us to miss out on great opportunities. If fear has limited your life and kept you stagnant, here are some great tools to use to outgrow your fear:

- Go to the library or go online and read everything you can about fear and facing your fear.

- Write about your fear, and if you are so inclined, share your writing with someone else to get feedback.

- Talk to someone about your fear to gain a different perspective.

- Seek professional help. If you are unable to resolve fears that become crippling and keep you stagnant, get some help. You deserve a good life free from anxiety and overwhelming fear.

- Join a support group in your community to gain support and affirmation from those who are experiencing the same challenges.

When I began my journey of healing, I was scared to death. Some questions that came to mind for me were: How is my life going to be now? What will I do? When will this pain ever go away? I remember literally having difficulty breathing. Later, I found that those who have experienced trauma often have difficulty breathing because they are constantly holding their breath waiting for the "other shoe to drop." Therefore, they never learn to relax and breathe deeply. This state is referred to as hyper-vigilance, which is an enhanced state of sensory sensitivity accompanied by an exaggerated intensity of behaviors whose purpose is to detect threats.

Hyper-vigilance is also accompanied by a state of increased anxiety, which can cause exhaustion.

One day shortly after I began my healing process over my divorce, I was in the car and in emotional pain, wondering how I was going to get through this difficult time in my life. I was crying out to God, telling Him how crushed I was, knowing that my marriage was over. The pain in my chest literally made it feel as if I could not breathe, as if I could not get enough air in my lungs. I asked God to help me breathe. Right after I said those words audibly in my car, a song called "Breathe" by Michael W. Smith came on the radio. The first words I heard were "This is the air I breathe." The song reminded me that my breath, my air, comes straight from God. He will give me air to breathe, and it will be He who strengthens me through the crushing pain of my divorce.

Exercise:

What are your biggest fears, and how have you coped with these fears in the past?

_____

_____

_____

_____

How have you allowed these fears to cripple, paralyze, or limit you?

_____

_____

_____

_____

What tools can you use now to begin walking through these fears?

_____

_____

_____

_____

Up to this point in your life, have you noticed any life preservers or signs that have been sent to you to help you on your path? What were they and how did they help you?

_____

_____

_____

_____

Be open and aware; look for the signs God is sending you as you walk toward the light and toward your freedom. Look for the life preserver and you will receive it, even when times are difficult and you feel you are in the dark. Fear is only fear! It is only a feeling and it will pass. Remember, you are surrounded by a loving God who will never leave you alone. Lean on the strength of those around you whom God puts in your life. While your journey is unique to you, others have been in similar situations and have found the light. You are not alone anymore.

FORGIVENESS: GIVING IT AND RECEIVING IT

"Forgiveness is the key that unlocks the door of resentment and the handcuffs of hatred. It is a power that breaks the chains of bitterness and the shackles of selfishness."

— **Corrie ten Boom**

While forgiveness is an idea and action that is difficult to describe in words, it is the only way you will find peace. Holding onto resentment is toxic and poisonous, and it hurts only you. But what does forgiveness mean? Here are some definitions of forgiveness that might be helpful as you begin letting go of old hurts (and maybe some new ones) on your path:

- To stop feeling anger toward (someone who has done something wrong): to stop blaming (someone).
- The act of forgiving or the state of being forgiven; willingness to forgive.

Forgiveness includes a conscious decision to release negative feelings like resentment and vengeance toward someone who has harmed you, even if the person does not deserve it. When you make the decision to forgive someone, it does not mean you agree with what he or she did, nor does it mean forgetting what happened. Forgiveness may help you repair a relationship; however, it does not mean you have to continue a relationship with someone because you have forgiven that person. If someone has abused you, it may not be healthy to continue participating in that relationship.

Know also that forgiveness can be a process. You may have to forgive someone in your head and heart many times before you are actually able to forgive someone fully. A good way to continue to forgive someone for something that continues to linger in your heart and mind is to remind yourself each time the resentment comes to the surface that you have forgiven him and pray that he have all the things in his life that you wish to have in your own. Practicing forgiveness produces so many benefits, including:

- Creates peace of mind from toxic anger

- Releases negative feelings

- Empowers us to move forward and heal

- Increases positive feelings

- Improves our health (anger and negative feelings negatively affect our immune system)

- Decreases stress

- Supports intimacy and positive skill-building in relationships

- Helps heal emotional wounds

- Cultivates empathy and compassion

Forgiveness is a gift you give to *yourself!* According to the Gospel, an offense calls for repentance and repentance calls for forgiveness. If you are the offender, do you truly understand and believe that you are forgiven? Unless you know you have been forgiven, it may be more difficult for you to forgive others in your life. In addition, according to Scripture, forgiveness includes:

- Forgiveness from God: We ask and He gives. This is when we go to God and ask Him to forgive our sins. If we are truly sincere and want to make a change, God will forgive us. *"If we confess our sins, he is faithful and just to forgive us our sins, and to cleanse us from all unrighteousness."* (1 John 1:9)

- Forgiveness from others: We ask and they may or may not give. When we hurt someone, we may go to that person to ask for forgiveness. However, we cannot control what he or she decides. *"Confess your faults one to another, and pray one for another, that ye may be healed. The effectual fervent prayer of a righteous man availeth much."* (James 5:16)

- Forgiveness to others: We forgive whether they ask or not. *"Then came Peter to him, and said, Lord, how oft shall my brother sin against me, and I forgive him? till seven times? Jesus saith unto him, I say not unto thee, Until seven times: but, Until seventy times seven."* (Matthew 18:21-22) We must forgive others and then, forgive more. Practicing endless forgiveness toward others regardless of whether they have asked our forgiveness or not is worth the effort.

You may believe the next bullet point should be forgiveness to ourselves. However, this is not true. Nowhere does God teach in His Word that one forgives oneself. We are forgiven by God and cleansed from our sin when we go to Him with a sincere heart. We ask others to forgive us and we forgive others. This covers all of the bases. If you still *feel* as if you are not forgiven, that is not true. If you are still feeling guilt for your wrongdoing, then consider whether you truly believe God forgave you. Also, remember that our actions have consequences. We may need to build back trust with someone. The person we wronged may not choose to have a relationship with us. There still may be a sentence to pay, such as jail time, community service, or a position or job we may have lost that we are unable to attain again.

I don't know of any more poignant story of forgiveness than that of Renee and Meagan Napier. As a mother, and human being, Renee Napier's strength after the death of her daughter, and her ability to forgive the person responsible, is what I consider a profound testament to God's ability to heal and to Renee's faith and true forgiveness.

On May 11, 2002, a drunk driver killed Renee's daughter, Meagan, and Meagan's friend, Lisa. The driver, Eric Smallridge, was convicted and sentenced to twenty-two years in prison. Although Renee was grieving the loss of her daughter, she came to forgive Eric, and in turn, Eric decided to make something positive out of his tragic mistake.

Less than two years after Meagan's death, Renee began giving DUI (Driving Under the Influence) presentations to audiences that included schools, the military, churches, and DUI offenders. Since 2004, over 100,000 people have heard Renee's presentation, during which she tells the story of Eric's decision to drink and drive and the ripple effect of consequences that resulted.

In April 2010, Eric was granted permission to join Renee in her speaking campaign. While still an inmate and bound by shackles, Eric captured the audience by boldly recounting the crash and his life in prison. Renee and Eric concluded the presentation with a compelling embrace. Eric was released from prison in November, 2012, because Renee requested of the judge to show leniency because Eric had apologized and truly repented.

Today, Renee is an award-winning speaker and remains very passionate about her mission to educate people about drinking and driving and the healing power of forgiveness. She is the President and Founder of The Meagan Napier Foundation, Incorporated, a 501(c)(3) non-profit organization.

In my own life, I have found that when going through turmoil and finding myself in situations that require extreme forgiveness, I have distanced myself from God because I think I know what is best rather than letting Him handle it. The battle has been with myself, in coming to an understanding and reconciling within myself when I feel I have been violated by others.

However, what if *you* are the one who needs to be forgiven? At any point in time, you can take responsibility for things you may have done or are doing and make amends. If you need to apologize to someone for your behavior, be sure you are ready to change the behavior, and then apologize. It can be very empowering to ask someone for his or her forgiveness. Do not be too proud to admit when you are wrong or when you need to apologize. Apologizing not only gives you internal freedom, but it makes you a great role model in your relationships.

One day I was babysitting two young boys who are brothers. While jumping on their trampoline, they began to bump into each other playfully, and as they continued in this manner, the older, bigger brother kicked the younger one hard enough to make him cry. This result, of course, stopped the jumping. I asked what happened from the younger one's point-of-view. Not surprisingly, he said his brother kicked him on purpose. The older one said he was sorry. I asked the younger one whether that made it all better. He said, "No" because he did not believe his brother really meant he was sorry.

After I talked with the older brother about how the younger one felt he was being picked on and that his older brother did not love him, the older brother realized the emptiness of his apology. Instead of being sincere and having a repentant heart, his empty words had hurt his younger brother. When a true, heartfelt exchange of apology and forgiveness happened, they were reconciled and went back to their play.

Exercise:

Here are some great questions about forgiveness to consider:

Do you believe you have a relationship of some kind with God? Describe this relationship.

_____

_____

_____

_____

Do you believe you have been forgiven? Why or why not? Is there anything for which you believe you have not been forgiven?

_____

_____

_____

_____

How has *not* forgiving others affected you and your peace of mind?

_____

_____

_____

_____

How has *not* forgiving others affected your relationship with God?

_____

_____

_____

_____

How can you start to forgive others and set yourself free?

_____

_____

_____

_____

After many years of feeling grief, resentment, and fear because I was sexually abused as a child, I knew I did not want to hold onto these crippling and negative feelings. I did not recognize at that time that I needed to forgive my perpetrator; I only knew that some kind of healing needed to happen. I wanted to have a relationship with my offender, but at the time that I began my healing, forgiveness was not a purposeful practice in my life.

As time went on, I experienced the grace of God's forgiveness. The more I believed and knew I was forgiven, the greater capacity I had to forgive others. The more you are forgiven, the more you are willing to forgive, and the greater capacity you have to show compassion and empathy toward others who have their own axes to grind and their own loads to carry. When it came down to me, I found that forgiveness equaled freedom.

Learn to forgive others, and to accept and receive the forgiveness that God has given you, and you will experience being set free.

"And when ye stand praying, forgive, if you have ought against any: that your Father also which is in heaven may forgive you your trespasses."

— Mark 11:25

You are forgiven, and you are loved, and when you realize and begin to acknowledge that you are forgiven, you will find it becomes easier to forgive others as well.

COURAGE IN RECOVERY

"Fear thou not; for I am with thee: be not dismayed; for I am thy God: I will strengthen thee; yea, I will help thee; yea, I will uphold thee with the right hand of my righteousness."

— Isaiah 41:10

At one of the most difficult times in my life when I finally acknowledged that I needed help, my first husband refused to pay for counseling so I began seeking work to pay for it. I became a Mary Kay Cosmetics consultant. Just when I felt things might be hopeless, I found camaraderie, a way to make money, and a host of amazing women who built me up and provided me with the training and skills I needed most.

I was so empowered by this experience, and at the same time, I began attending a different church, which coincidentally offered free counseling! The counseling at my new church turned out to be an ideal fit for me, and I was able to develop further my spiritual foundation and learn even more about how much God loves me!

At the same time, I found a spiritual mentor who taught me how to read the Bible and how to cope with what I believe is a broken, sinful, and fallen world, and I found that God was with me every step of the way. As my life began shifting and changing, my joy became more full and my anger became less.

Yes, it is true that recovery is painful and you must leap with both feet into the unknown. Recovery takes courage because you are moving into an area of uncertainty and out of your comfort zone. You may find your recovery requires a large majority of time and attention in order for you to get well, including taking time off work and focusing on your emotional, physical, and spiritual conditions.

Exercise:

Do you believe you are worth whatever you may have to do to recover? Why or why not?

_____

_____

_____

_____

_____

Do you believe you are worth the time and effort you may need to put yourself first and find the recovery you seek? How much time do you think your recovery might take?

_____

_____

_____

_____

_____

In what ways are you already courageous? What things have you already done to begin the recovery process?

_____

_____

_____

_____

_____

Where will you seek out help so you can get support for your recovery?

_____

_____

_____

_____

_____

What are you willing to do today, right now, to begin your recovery journey?

_____

_____

_____

_____

SUMMARY

When you make the decision to recover from whatever your ailment—abuse, trauma, domestic violence, addiction, or even a broken heart—you will find that the resources you require will be put in your path. At times you may feel this is not true, but if you are steadfast and keep asking and looking, you will be provided with what you need. Do not give up if you feel things are not moving fast enough or if you are having a hard time finding the services or solutions you need. The answers and resources will come when you keep an open mind and begin seeking help and taking action.

It will be important for you to find help with those you can truly trust, so take your time and acknowledge that it is a journey, not a destination. If you have gained help but do not feel the help you have found is a good fit for you, continue looking until you are able to get your needs met in a way that feels right for you.

You will need to walk through your fear to get to the other side. Recovery takes courage, but you do not have to walk the path alone. Find others to relate to who have been through similar situations. Share with others about your experiences and read about others who have been where you are. So many stories are in your local library and on the Internet about ordinary people who found extraordinary strength of spirit to survive the worst circumstances.

These stories can give you hope, lift you up, and help you continue moving forward when things get difficult. As time goes on and you begin to heal, you will not only learn how to ask for forgiveness, but you will also learn how to forgive others and to let go and let God.

Encouraging others is another character asset we must develop. Encouragement is such a gift. When someone has been through so much, whether it is sexual trauma, emotional or physical abuse, or some sort of addiction, validation can mean comfort, but unfortunately, it is not often given. At times, no one else can do the work necessary for us to survive. We have to do the work and we realize it is truly an inside job.

During the time I was recovering from my abuse, my pastor told a story one day in church that really demonstrated this idea to me.

Two men went hunting for quail. Hunting can require a lot of waiting and observing your surroundings, and at one point, they noticed an unattended bird's nest in the field, which contained three eggs, one of which was beginning to hatch! After quite some time, they finally saw the chick's beak and some of its head peeking out of the shell. The task of this chick breaking out of the shell seemed so long and tedious to the pair of hunters. After a long while, they decided to "help" the baby chick by breaking away parts of the shell to make it easier for the chick to come out.

They were like chick-hatching heroes because they were there to offer a helping hand in the process, and the chick became free from its shell in no time. It tried to move around the new world outside of its shell, but the baby chick did not seem to gain strength. In fact, the chick seemed to be growing weaker and weaker as time went on. The two hunters began to realize that the chick was dying, but they could not do anything to help it, and the chick, in fact, did die. What they learned later was that the time and energy it would have taken for the chick to break its way out of the shell was necessary for the chick to fill its tiny little lungs with air. Not allowing the chick to do all of the work by itself made it impossible for the chick's lungs to develop properly.

As much as it can hurt us to watch others struggle for survival, and as much as we may want them to hurry up and heal, no one can go through recovery for someone else. Each person is responsible for doing his or her own work and putting in the time it takes to heal. What we can do is to love them, encourage them, hear them, and validate them. Remember what you think might be helpful, may not be. Try to discern what you are supposed to do, and when in doubt, ask what you can do and then, do that.

A TREASURE AND A PEARL

Being able to reach out for help, to gain an advocate, or some other kind of help, is a gift. We all need each other and a sense of connectedness to heal. We need the gift of relationships with other people and with God because we cannot cope with life or recover from our pain by ourselves. Sometimes it is hard to trust people, but we can always learn, and we can count on God never to forsake us. God knows you are valuable and He loves you. He sent his Son Jesus to die for you and to forgive you for all of your sins, and He wants to connect with you. For myself, I decided to *accept* His invitation and the gift He was trying to offer me my whole life. My blinders have been removed, and I have no more fear about what people might think of me for deciding to enter into a relationship with Jesus. Accept the truth and His invitation to you. His gifts are waiting for you too.

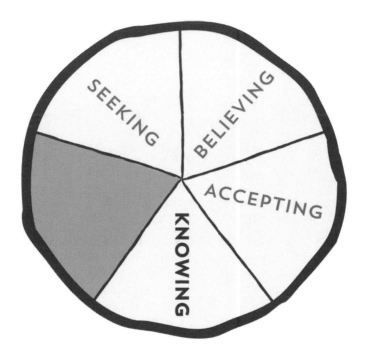

Knowing: To possess knowledge, information, or understanding.

Chapter Four

TRANSITIONING
WITH HOPE

"Knowledge is power."

— Sir Francis Bacon

Transition and change are certainly a natural part of life. As you begin to understand what it is you need to have, be, and do in relation to thriving and living a hopeful and inspired life, rather than just surviving, you may find yourself in a state of transition that may seem constant. Changes in work, relationships, health, finances, and environment may all occur as you begin growing and healing.

CHANGE HAPPENS

Throughout your life, at least in the culture that has been created in the United States, anticipatory changes occur that naturally create transitions, such as going through the developmental stages of infancy, being a toddler, youth, adolescence, young adulthood, mid-life, and the golden years.

In addition, societal norms create change and transition as you begin maturing, such as: going to college, getting married, having a family, and eventually retiring. All of these natural transitions create change, sometimes even paramount change. For example, when a young person grows up and goes to college, while this is a huge life change for the young person, it may also create the feeling of "empty-nest" syndrome for the parents who now must begin redefining themselves because being parents is no longer taking on the same role.

Transitions may even create new and uncomfortable feelings, like depression and confusion, and they may instigate a need to find other outlets in which the parent may again feel more needed and useful. Some parents get pets or find other activities to offset this life change, or they lean on other friends and family who have had similar experiences. Divorce is another example of a huge transition that affects not only the primary relationship between partners and children, if there are any, but also relationships with other family members and even friends.

Change happens all the time, and it is normal if you have a pulse and are alive, but it can also create stress. Everyone feels stress at some time, whether it is at work, in family, when making decisions, or when major life events occur, such as illness, the death of a loved one, divorce, or changes in responsibility at home or work. Job loss, increased job responsibility, a promotion, the birth of a baby, or moving are other examples of change that can cause stress.

There is positive stress, which is referred to as eustress, and negative stress, which is referred to as distress. Both can affect your body and your mental wellbeing. While each individual person has his or her own unique response to stress, some responses are similar and create similar feelings including:

- Feelings of being out of control

- Inability to meet your own and others' expectations while under stress

- Uncertainty

- Guilt over inability to perform at your best

- Inability to keep commitments

Stress management is very important when going through change. Your ability or lack thereof to diffuse your own stress level will dictate whether *your stress has you, or you have stress.* Here are some tips to diffuse your stress:

- Eat well and exercise. When you eat junk food, it tears down your immune system and can actually cause illness. In addition, stress can cause you to experience low self-worth and deplete dopamine and serotonin, which directly affect the pleasure center in your brain.

- Good, healthy food and regular exercise can keep your immune system running at its optimum level and can stabilize the serotonin and dopamine in your brain. Take a walk, do some deep breathing and stretching, or choose some form of physical activity to release the stress from your body.

- Practice a hobby. Do you already have one? Then make time to enjoy it! If you do not have a hobby, get one. Write a list of the things you might like to try, and begin doing them to see whether they are things you might enjoy. Hobbies can relieve stress and distract your mind from stressful situations.

- Engage in social activities. Pick up the phone and call people you care about, spend an evening out with friends, and/or join a club or social organization, which can all help alleviate stress.

- Pray and meditate. If you do not know how, you can always learn. Prayer and meditation are great ways to refocus and get centered with God and to relax and gain peace of mind.

- Read a good book, like this one! Find inspiring and positive reading material that can help lift you up and raise your spirits.

- Watch a good movie, or better yet, watch a good movie with a friend!

Exercise:

Have you been able to diffuse your stress in the past when life changes have created stress for you? How so?

_____

_____

_____

_____

What are some new tools you can use to support your wellbeing when you are experiencing stress?

_____

_____

_____

_____

How have you personally been affected by eustress (positive stress) and distress (negative stress) in your life?

_____

_____

_____

_____

What other thoughts do you have about how you can better handle changes when they occur?

_____

_____

_____

_____

When you are experiencing change and have stress as a result, it can feel overwhelming and scary. Practicing new tools and strategies to intervene on your own behalf when you experience significant change can help you effectively cope with stress and feel empowered and competent. Remember that feelings are only feelings. They will pass, and as long as you take affirmative action and seek solutions, rather than allowing the stress of change to incapacitate you, you will be well on your way to moving forward.

YOU ARE NOT YOUR CIRCUMSTANCES

When I was going through my divorce, a huge part of my identity, up until that point, had been that of a wife. My future, all my plans, my dreams and fantasies had all been related to being a wife. I had no idea what to do at that point because I felt that if I were not a wife after all, I was nothing. What I found over the course of my journey was that my identity is not "what I do" but rather it is "who I am." My identity is my spirit, my soul, and my essence.

You see, I am not a victim of my circumstances. If I have victory over my circumstances, then I am not a victim of circumstances. If I see myself as a divorcee, or a laid-off employee, or that my identity is directly attached to whatever life change has occurred, then

I become a victim of that change. Once I was able to understand and acknowledge this realization, I could make choices to identify with my positive character attributes, such as: I am powerful, I have choices, I am honest, and I have integrity. These character attributes are mine, whether I am married or divorced, whether I have employment or am laid off. No circumstances dictate my worth or who I am any longer.

Exercise:

Have you thought about whether you believe the roles you provide in your life are "who you are"? How so?

_____

_____

_____

_____

Who are you really? While it may be true that you perform roles in your life at home, work, and in general, what are the good things about you that make up the essence of who you really are?

_____

_____

_____

_____

Now that you know you are not the roles you perform, how can you begin to develop and support the real you, your soul, and your spirit?

_____

_____

_____

_____

Do you understand now that you must begin to identify yourself as something more than the roles you play? If you believe you are only the roles you perform, when they end or change, you will be left with nothing, and you will be in the position of being a victim of your circumstances.

The truth is that *you* are creating your life, and you are not your past or the roles you have chosen to take on. You decide to make responsible choices for your future. Begin identifying who you are by the character attributes and positive qualities you possess. You are unique, wonderful, and amazing, and God loves you. You are not the roles you have chosen to take on in your life. As your roles change, be flexible. Continue to acknowledge the wonderful things about you and build on those.

THINGS HAPPEN FOR A REASON

"Blessed are they that mourn: for they shall be comforted."

— Matthew 5:4

It is hard to see the forest for the trees during difficult times in our lives, and sometimes we just cannot get through stuff without getting some sort of external help. There is no shame in reaching out for help when we need it. The shame is when we choose not to reach out for help when we need it. When we become unwilling to reach out, we stunt our own growth, create the environment for untold suffering, and can even compound our problems.

While going through my divorce, I *had* to decide to get some help because I did not know how to be divorced, how to cope with my feelings, or even how to function from day to day. I had given up my entire identity to my marriage and needed a complete emotional rebuild from the ground up. After working with a counselor, I learned about the stages of grief that applied to my divorce. I had always thought the stages of grief only applied to death.

Acknowledging and understanding my grief was horribly depressing because it occurred to me that I had a lot of work ahead of me and that it was going to take a lot of time. After my healing journey from my childhood sexual abuse, the last thing I wanted to do was deal with the grief and loss associated with my divorce! On the other hand, just as important was the desire I had to get my joy back, and I *knew* God could bring me through my pain if only I could muster up the courage to continue my journey.

The loss of anticipation of growing old with someone, my livelihood, and my home; the loss of the idea that my children would have two loving, married parents; and other losses, including self-esteem, trust, mutual friends, someone I *thought* was a friend, my reality and identity as a wife, my title as Mrs. and my husband's last name; and financial loss all weighed heavily on my heart.

Even more painful was the loss of the concept in my mind and heart that marriage was permanent, the loss of the vows I lived by, and the loss of the promise I made to my husband, God, and myself. And what about the children? As parents, we hurt when our children hurt, and I could see that the divorce was significantly affecting my children. It was so difficult to serve my children well because I was not well myself. At times, I was unable to put my own grief aside to help them with their grief and this was heartbreaking for me.

Even now after several years, it is still such a huge loss, and with each passing day, I am coming to the realization that even the marriage of which I am grieving the loss is not the marriage I thought I had. This is why having supportive friends and family is so important.

There may be times in your life when you feel so overwhelmed you will want to petition God to make the pain go away, but you will also understand that He will give you the strength you need to handle it. By getting through these hard times, you are in the unique and important position to help others going through their own trials because of your experiences. Here are some great tools and strategies to help you on your healing journey:

- Find one person you can talk to whom you consider a mentor. Maybe this person is someone who knows you already and has a knowledge base of your circumstances. Ask him or her to help you assess the situation and provide guidance if necessary. Share your feelings and concerns and receive important support in the process.

- Look ahead for any predictable circumstances you might face in the near future so you are not caught off-guard when the time comes. Plan ahead whenever possible and do not bury your head in the sand. Learn how to be accountable and deal with situations rather than avoiding them because change is inevitable.

- Have realistic expectations. Read and learn about things that happen in the natural course of life. For instance: what happens during menopause, what happens when kids leave home, how to save money for retirement and determine how much money you will need.

- Realize that people cope with change differently. If you have difficulty coping with change, do not beat yourself up about it; rather, begin seeking solutions so you know you are prepared and more flexible when change occurs.

- As previously stated, practice self-care: eat well and drink plenty of fluids, do not isolate yourself, and keep in contact regularly with people you can count on and trust.

- Practice healthy activities that make you feel happy and joyful.

- If you are a parent or caregiver to someone else, make sure you have time off to recharge and refill your cup. Take time off from your daily routine. You may have to pay to have someone to do what you cannot get done, such as mow the lawn or clean the house, to free up some time. If you can afford it, make having free time a priority.

- Cooking may be overwhelming so ask a friend to go out to dinner with you, or for that friend to visit and bring you a meal.

- Ask for help!

Things will never stay the same because change is the one sure thing. Expect things to change; kids get older, we get older, our bodies change, our circumstances change, our work changes, and our priorities change. Change can happen *to* us, or we can choose to roll *with* the change. We can be the victim or the victor. Which will you choose?

Exercise:

Are there issues in your life that continue to cause you grief and loss? What are they?

_____

_____

_____

_____

How can you move from the position of a victim into a victor?

_____

_____

_____

_____

Which of the tools and strategies discussed in this chapter can you utilize to help you become a victor?

_____

_____

_____

_____

Changes do not happen to hurt or punish you, but it can be difficult to remember that everything happens for a reason, especially during hard times. If we ultimately believe God is for us and not against us, then we will experience more peace about the things happening around us because we will remember once again that everything happens for a reason. Many times we ask, "Why me? Why this? Why now?" We may not get the answers, but just knowing there is a reason can make it bearable, and finding out what the reason is can be exciting and builds faith and trust.

Sitting on the pity pot only supports misery. Taking a proactive approach, however, can help you stay in the solution. For example, it is the difference between asking, "What did I do to deserve cancer?" and "What is it I am going to learn as a result of this trial, and how will I be able to help others as a result?"

STATISTICS ARE NOT THE WHOLE STORY

I feel compelled to discuss the idea of statistics in recovering from adversity and other life events and changes. If you live by information provided by statistics, then you support the statistics. When you support the statistics, you, in fact, become them and potentially lose faith in the power of God and His ability to heal you.

Statistics are often the compilation of subjective measurement tools, and you can mistakenly count on statistics rather than relying on your own common sense and ability to make informed decisions, especially when these same statistics are commonly accepted in our society.

If I had allowed statistics to predict my future, I never would have gotten married the second time because, statistically, we were destined to fail. If I believed the statistics that Lindsey, my daughter, had an 80 percent chance to die, I never would have had the faith to believe she was supposed to live.

Do not allow statistics to keep you from succeeding! If you never knew the chances were slim and you carried on as though they were completely possible, you could actually help to create a shift in the statistics. Do you want to be a statistic changer or a statistic follower? You can allow statistics to define you or you can work even harder at changing them! The script is in your hand, so write it well, hope for the best, and have faith always. Believe that everything happens according to God's plan.

DIVINE APPOINTMENTS

Have you ever had a day when things just started to get to you and you needed a breath of fresh air to get a new perspective? One day, I decided to multi-task so I could take a thirty-minute break, and my car needed an oil change, so I used the time to go to Jiffy Lube. It was right down the street from my job and it only takes about twenty minutes so it seemed like a good use of my time. The building has a little lobby with coffee and tea and magazines to help pass the time, so I got a cup of tea and sat down to relax.

A woman came in behind me and sat down as well. I was not in the mood to chitchat, so I kept my nose in the magazine I was reading. After a twenty-minute wait, I noticed the staff had not even started working on my car yet, which was unusual. Apparently, the woman next to me noticed the same thing because she asked me whether it was usual for it to take this long for oil to be changed. She said she was in a hurry, and I responded that I, too, was in a hurry and was on break from work. I told her I am usually able to get my oil change quite quickly.

When she asked me where I worked, I told her that I worked down the street at the local hospital. She had an expression of interest on her face, despite her sunglasses, and she mentioned that her husband had spent a good amount of time there as a patient recently and asked whether I knew him. I answered that I did not really know him, but I had spoken to him on occasion while he was in the hospital. She told me he had passed away and asked me whether I knew that he had died. I told her that I had heard he passed away and that I was very sorry for her loss.

She took off her dark sunglasses and asked me, "Did he ask about going home a lot, or did he mention how he didn't want to be there in the hospital?" This was such an interesting question to me because I could see in her eyes the pain and grief of knowing her husband wanted to come home and didn't like being in the hospital, but also that he needed to be there to get better.

I answered her question with a short story of my encounter with this man; I remember entering into his room, letting him know who I was, and then I noticed he had his Bible opened up on the tray table next to his bed. I mentioned to him that I noticed his Bible and asked whether he had a favorite verse. He began to recite from memory several consecutive verses from his favorite place in the Bible.

It was obvious that this man loved the Lord and the Word of God. He clearly spent time memorizing it. His voice changed when he spoke the verses; it was usually soft and frail, but when he recited his favorite verses, he became alive and his voice became strong and full of joy. Being a fellow believer in Jesus, we spoke for a short time about our love for God.

The woman began to cry and said that sounded just like her husband. Then I told her I had asked him whether there was anything we could do to make his stay more comfortable. He said no, but that he prayed his stay in the hospital would somehow change someone's life. The woman began to tear up and said once again that that sounded just like her husband.

Our conversation in the Jiffy Lube that day was a catalyst for this woman to experience beautiful memories of her husband. However, these had not been her experiences with her husband before he died. What was amazing to her was that her husband had late stage Alzheimer's, yet he was able to recite so much from his Bible.

I told her that, being unaware of her husband's Alzheimer's, I had spoken to him like anyone else because I had no idea he could not remember most things, but oh, how he could remember the love he had for God! The words from his Bible were engraved in his memory and heart, and his ability to recite them was how he fulfilled his hope that God would use his stay at the hospital to change someone's life.

The delay this woman and I experienced while getting our oil changes was clearly a divine appointment the Lord had for us. We were meant to meet so I could tell her the story of the day I spoke to her husband, so the story would reveal to her the confidence her husband still had inside his own heart about his ability to spread the Good News of the love of Jesus, even though his brain was affected by Alzheimer's.

I know this man changed at least one life while he was sick—mine! The fact that his story is being told again now is a testament that we can change lives by the way we live, and we can continue to change lives even after we are gone by the example we leave behind us.

I know this divine appointment blessed both the woman and me. I hope it blesses you in some way. If nothing else, when your oil change is taking longer than expected, look for the blessing of that delay. Not only will your oil be changed, but maybe even your life!

SURVIVING THE FIRE

I love sitting around a campfire, and it is always so amazing to gaze into its flames. So many lessons can be learned from fire. Have you ever noticed that somehow when people sit around a fire in the dark, discussions can become so much more deep and intimate?

One evening, my husband Frank and I lit a fire in a small firepit. It was not a big fire, but every so often, the flames grew with the soft breeze. The heat from the fire was desirable on this particularly cool evening, and we had some family members over who didn't really want to come outside in the cool air; however, when they saw the fire, it drew them out.

A few kids were in our crowd that night, and I thought maybe they would enjoy some leftover bubbles from a wedding we had recently attended. The kids began to blow the bubbles all over the yard, but then something interesting happened. They began to blow the bubbles near the fire, and I noticed the bubbles floated high up above the fire. The other bubbles in the yard away from the fire descended to the ground and then popped. But why did some bubbles float high above the flames? Now I was curious.

When I asked everyone to blow the bubbles directly into the fire, something unexpected happened. The bubbles were caught up in the heat of the fire and the heat grabbed the bubbles and drew them up above the fire so they could float away without popping. This made me think about the fire in our own lives and the heat that fire brings.

If I put my hand in the fire, it will burn, yet I am still drawn to the fire on some level. The heat also keeps the bubbles from being destroyed by the fire itself, but there would be no heat without the fire. The bubbles are delicate, but not so delicate that they would be popped when encountering the heat.

The painful events that happen in our lives are just like the bubbles. Whether they be of our own doing, someone else's doing, or just the plain old circumstances of life, the very thing that is painful is what gives us opportunities to learn, grow, and rise above the circumstances in life (the fire) that bring us pain.

Instead of popping when blown toward the fire, the bubble is swept away to a safe place above the fire. Similarly, human beings are resilient; when we are weak, we are strong. Hope gives us strength. It brings us to a place where we rise above the pain of life, and it allows us to learn and grow from our experiences. We realize in our weakness that we are strong. I love the bubbles, and all the visuals, the concrete pictures and experiences that God sends our way if we but just look.

Exercise:

What are some examples of you rising above the fire in your life?

_____

_____

_____

_____

In what ways have you been given opportunities to learn and grow through experiencing the fire?

_____

_____

_____

_____

How has God lifted you up to safety during the times you were experiencing the fire?

_____

_____

_____

Sometimes, others' fires are what we must rise above. Sometimes, those we love most must go through the fire while we stand witness to their experiences in it. Has this ever happened to you? Have you ever been burned by the fire of another and lifted up into the safety of God's loving arms?

For most of my life, I had never had the experience of anyone dying right before me, although I had seen people on their death-beds and had seen people who were recently deceased. Then my sister-in-law was diagnosed with breast cancer and fought a long and hard battle. For several years, she seemed to beat it altogether, but it came back and metastasized in many areas of her body. Her attitude of living in spite of the cancer was so inspiring.

The family received many calls over a period of about three years, and each time it was believed she would be leaving this earth. Miraculously, each time she beat the odds, went home from the hospital, and returned to her life.

However, this time when my brother called and told the family that hospice was involved, we somehow knew the time was near and that she would die. I immediately got on a plane to go see her and be there for my brother since I could only imagine how difficult it was for him to experience the death of his beloved.

When I got there, my sister-in-law was sleeping, but I was told she had been up laughing and talking the night before with family and friends and also just a couple of hours before I arrived. I thought for sure she would wake up and we would have a wonderful conversation, but she was so tired. When she did seem to wake up, she was very groggy, so I am not sure she really knew who I was when we spoke. It was not really a conversation but a few words in greeting. She was in the hospital bed in her living room and planned to be there until she died. She seemed to slip away so fast and every hour she was given morphine for the pain.

The hospice nurse came the next morning and talked to us about her condition and what to expect. She also very reverently gave my sister-in-law a sponge bath and told us that while my sister-in-law may not be able to talk, hearing was the last of the senses to go, and that she could most likely hear us.

The conversation I planned to have with her would have to be a one-way conversation it seemed since I was the only one talking and praying. As the day went on, it was evident that she was passing away. Her breath became especially shallow and my brother sat close by, lovingly stroking her hair and her face. I stood at the foot of the bed and noticed how her body was becoming less and less "full." To be in the presence of someone's last breath on this earth, I must say, was very impactful for me.

As I stood there looking at her, an obvious and immediate change occurred in her appearance. It was as if I saw her body go from alive to hollow and dead in a split second. She was now in heaven with God. Her body, which had once carried her soul, became an empty vessel. This was the first time I had actually experienced someone dying. I have heard people talk about their belief that the human soul leaves the body when it dies, but to see the difference in the body's appearance when the soul is present and then leaves was so incredible. God revealed to me in that moment that the time we spend in this life and in our bodies is temporary until it is the soul's time to leave. I know my sister-in-law loved Jesus and had a relationship with Him and so her relationship with Him continues in a different place. When it became clear to everyone that she was gone, the tears began to flow over the reality of her death.

This experience added to the foundation of my faith. It has helped me see that having and embracing a relationship with Jesus is such a comfort when things like death occur in our lives. We can still embrace the real and true love of God when we are in pain, even during times of pain greater than we can ever imagine. Even during times when our hearts are in pain, when someone dies, or when a relationship that we desire dies, we can rely on the love of God to see us through and have hope that He will restore our joy.

WOUNDED HEARTS HEAL: SCARS ARE BEAUTIFUL

"There is something beautiful about all scars of whatever nature.
A scar means the hurt is over, the wound is closed
and healed, done with."

— Harry Crews

Whether you are experiencing the feelings of going through divorce, surviving abuse or trauma, or going through a major life transition or change, there is always an opportunity for your heart to mend. Your emotional scars and even your physical scars are beautiful. Your scars are your testament of courage and are part of your story. Consider that when you are aware of your scars, you know you are alive and that you have survived. Though many people may feel ashamed of their scars, beauty comes from within. Your emotional, physical, and spiritual wellbeing is an inside job.

You are not your body, and God knows just how beautiful you are because God knows your heart. I was quite surprised when a Mary Kay consultant told me once that I had beautiful skin and did not really need to wear makeup. This happened at a time when I was considering discontinuing wearing makeup altogether for the first time in my life.

I had worn makeup for many years because Max had told me that I needed to and that I was not attractive without it. This wounded my heart so much, and I did not realize just how much it hurt me until my husband Frank kept pointing out how beautiful he thought I was even on bad hair days! He reminded me that I was already beautiful to the ones who love me—my God and himself—and that I did not have to do anything to change the way I look to receive their love.

Exercise:

How do your emotional, physical, or spiritual scars affect your feelings about yourself?

_____

_____

_____

_____

What are the messages you have accepted about yourself and your scars that no longer serve you?

_____

_____

_____

What are some things you can say to yourself when you recognize that you are sending yourself old messages that are negative and unloving?

_____

_____

_____

_____

Whom do you have in your life who loves you just the way you are?

_____

_____

_____

_____

Do you believe God loves you just the way you are? Why or why not?

_____

_____

_____

_____

SUMMARY

Change can be difficult and uncomfortable, but it is also necessary to develop our character and to grow. Change can also create stress, so it very important to be vigilant about practicing good stress management skills, especially when you are going through change and transitions in your life.

Remember, no matter what is going on around you, you are not your circumstances and you are not a victim. At any time, you can make different choices that will then change your circumstances.

Identify the good things about you and recognize that everything happens for a reason. This realization is how you will continue to grow using change as a catalyst.

Keep your eyes and heart open for the divine appointments that God has set in place for you. You do not want to miss them because you are so caught up in what "seems" to be happening.

Remember that like bubbles above a fire, every painful event you weather makes you stronger and helps you grow. You are resilient and your emotional, physical, and spiritual scars are beautiful. Over time and through God's love, wounded hearts truly heal. The famous poet Rumi said, *"The wound is the place where the light enters in."* I have found this saying to be so true for myself.

A TREASURE AND A PEARL

You are beautiful and you can heal from your wounds. Everything happens for a reason, and though the lessons may not be clear at first, as you pray and get to *know* God, more will be revealed to you. Some tools that helped me better understand my relationship with Jesus included having someone walk alongside me and teach me how to relate to God, reading my Bible, and learning about the Trinity: God, Jesus, and the Holy Spirit. My journey has not been an easy one, but I want to continue learning, and I know that if I want a relationship with God, I must go to Jesus in prayer. Putting myself in places like church, where there are like-minded people, has also helped me on my path. Even though I know it will take a lifetime to grow my relationship with God, I cannot wait to find out what will happen next!

Embracing: To support (a belief, theory, or change) willingly and enthusiastically.

Chapter Five

LEADING WITH HOPE

"Blessed be God, even the Father of our Lord Jesus Christ, the Father of mercies, and the God of all comfort; Who comforteth us in all our tribulation, that we may be able to comfort them which are in any trouble, by the comfort wherewith we ourselves are comforted of God."

— 2 Corinthians 1:3-4

LEADING WITH HOPE

We are all leaders in our own right. As participants in the many roles we play in our lives—parents, spouses, employees, and friends—we lead and influence those around us every day. What child does not look up to and count on her parents for guidance, love, and support? What spouse in some way does not value the guidance, opinion, affirmation, and affection of his or her mate? What employee does not look to his employer for training, skill building, and motivation? Don't we all at times count on the opinions and listening ears of our friends?

Even hard-to-get-along-with people are looking to others for leadership, but just because we are all leaders does not necessarily mean we are good ones. Have you ever had an employer who discounted or degraded his/her employees or even treated employees badly in front of other employees, or worse still, in front of customers?

Good leadership can be a buffer and a catalyst for difficult change and can shepherd others into the hard places. When someone is truly leading, he emulates hope, and this hope creates an environment of safety. Leaders who are hopeful or hope-filled usher others toward the light. Hope-filled leaders are embraced by those they lead and people gravitate toward them. They are, in essence, a beacon and draw people to them like a magnet, and they light the path for others in their everyday interactions.

While others may have experienced dictatorships in their leaders, a joyful and exciting tugging toward accomplishment and reciprocal respect happens when a hope-filled leader is at the helm. A natural evolution occurs that includes mutual respect and the understanding that everybody counts and is equally important; problem-solving becomes inclusive and proactive as a direct result. Hope-filled leaders are natural mentors and can humbly admit when they are wrong.

"Darkness cannot drive out darkness; only light can do that. Hate cannot drive out hate; only love can do that."

— Martin Luther King, Jr.

Martin Luther King, Jr. is one such example of a hope-filled leader. An American clergyman, activist, humanitarian, and leader in the African-American Civil Rights movement, King is best known for his work to advance rights for all, using non-violent civil disobedience. He helped organize the 1963 March on Washington, during which time he delivered his "I Have a Dream" speech. He became one of the greatest leaders and orators in history, but it was his message of hope that was most profound of all.

You see, Martin Luther King, Jr. believed that justice and respect belonged to everyone, and that dignity and respect are God-given rights for all. He believed that hatred and bitterness were poisonous and that everyone was created equal, and he put his very own life on the line to help those who could not help themselves. He gave them hope, he gave them comfort, and he modeled mercy despite the horrendous acts to which African-Americans had been subjected.

Martin Luther King, Jr. was awarded the Presidential Medal of Freedom and the Congressional Gold Medal. In 1986, a U.S. federal holiday was established and hundreds of streets throughout the United States were named in his honor. A memorial statue on the National Mall opened to the public in 2011 commemorating Martin Luther King, Jr.

Exercise:

How are you a hope-filled leader?

_____

_____

_____

_____

_____

How do you share your light and love with others in your role as a leader at home, at work, and with friends?

_____

_____

_____

_____

What are some things you can do to model mercy and give others comfort in your role as a leader at home, at work, and with friends?

_____

_____

_____

_____

LEADING AND FOLLOWING

All hope-filled and skilled leaders also know how to follow. Knowing how to follow is mandatory in order to develop compassion and understanding. Whether you are a follower or a leader, be forever mindful that you are working in tandem with your Creator. Keep Him behind the steering wheel and do your best to remain in the passenger seat. If you find yourself struggling, remember He is in charge. Keep fresh in your mind that you are responsible for being an example of hope and of God's love in all of your leadership activities. 1 Peter 3:15 states: *"But sanctify the Lord God in your hearts: and be ready always to give an answer to every man that asketh you a reason of the hope that is in you with meekness and fear."*

We are all following others, and we all have others following us whether or not we are aware of it. You are teaching the people around you, especially your children, valuable lessons through the modeling of your behavior both as a follower and a leader. What are you teaching those around you? Here are some important thoughts to consider:

- Is your message "Do as I say, not as I do"? If it is, how can you change it?

- Is your approach gentle and does it promote mutual respect? If not, how can you make it so?

- Do you cultivate an environment of safety and hope? When faced with issues, such as cussing, drinking alcohol, using drugs, and verbal and emotional abuse, do you tolerate such behavior or seek to stop or change it?

The apple rarely falls far from the tree, which means our behavior directly teaches others, especially those who are impressionable like children, how to think and behave.

The lyrics from a country song I heard on the radio really drove home this idea for me. In essence, it said that a father found that his young son was smoking cigarettes, and when he asked his son why he would do such a thing, the son told his father he wanted to be just like him. The man had an epiphany in that moment that he did not want his son to be like him. The father later saw his son praying. When he asked him where he learned to pray, his son said, "From you, Dad." Sometimes in life, we may not even know whether we are the student or the teacher! Our children will learn both good and bad lessons from us so we need to be aware and vigilant about striving to be the best we can be.

How do you want to show up in your relationships with your children, spouse, employer, and friends? Do you want to be negative, self-centered, impatient, unkind, and unloving? Or do you want to be hope-filled, of service to others, patient, kind, and loving? It is *your* choice, and you can change your behavior in any given moment. Lean on God and let Him mold you and help you become your very best. Let go of control and be willing to follow and embrace God's direction.

By this point in *The Hope Factor*, you have developed and practiced tools to begin trusting the process that allows you to surrender to God and His will for you. While you may still be unclear about where you are going, you can still be obedient. Following and obediently trusting where God leads you is much more productive than being clear about where you are going and being disobedient. Personally, I have found that I would much rather be obedient and not know where I am going than disobedient and know where I am.

Years ago, God nudged me through prayer to become a professional speaker and to write this book. My spiritual walk and the messages I was receiving from the Bible repeatedly confirmed this new vocation for me. Through my awareness and understanding of Psalm 68:11, which says, "*The Lord gave the word: great was the company of those that published it,*" I felt both confirmation and affirmation that not only was I to follow my calling, but that God would send me an army to publish my book and audiences to hear its message. I am not required to do everything on my own, only to follow God's lead. There will always be someone to support us and help us accomplish the tasks that God wants accomplished.

Matthew 7:7 states, "*Ask, and it shall be given you; seek, and ye shall find; knock, and it shall be opened unto you.*" When you are leading or following, you may not always be moving. Sometimes, following means waiting, listening, and being patient until the right answers come, or until you feel called to take action. If you are someone who feels compelled to act constantly, do not let the habit of taking action deter you from being still in order to hear the message(s) of God. He speaks to each of us differently in ways we can personally understand and experience. He speaks to me the way He knows I need to be spoken to. Just as each child is different and unique and needs to be treated as such, so, too, does God treat us.

Exercise:

Are you able to follow or do you have difficulty letting go of the steering wheel? Explain why.

_____

_____

_____

_____

What are some of the lessons your behavior is teaching your children, spouse, employer, and friends?

_____

_____

_____

_____

How do you suppose your ability to follow (or lack thereof) has affected your ability to listen to and follow God's plan for your life?

_____

_____

_____

_____

What is your calling? How have you been nudged to follow your calling?

———————————————————————————
———————————————————————————
———————————————————————————
———————————————————————————

How can you now begin taking steps to follow your calling if you have not already?

———————————————————————————
———————————————————————————
———————————————————————————
———————————————————————————

SPEAKING AND SHARING YOUR MESSAGE OF HOPE

We are all in the unique position, if we believe in ourselves enough, to share our experiences and stories with others because we have something valuable to say. Your testimony and your life lessons when shared with others become hope. There is something special and unique about you, and every trial, tribulation, and triumph you have experienced is an opportunity to share how God has helped you to overcome it. Maybe you have experienced a problem such as addiction, sexual abuse, domestic violence, or poverty. Maybe you have experienced more than one of these issues in your life. Now is your opportunity to speak up, be heard, and share the solution found in God's loving arms.

There is a light inside of you that shines like no one else's. Why would you want to hide it when so many are suffering without it?

God wants you to share your life lessons and your message with others. In this way, you can be of maximum service to Him. When you have come through the darkness and been comforted by the loving light of God, you have been given the greatest gift of all, but you cannot keep it to yourself; you must give it away.

WICKED

I am a Midwestern gal, and for most of my life, I lived in a place where the possibility of a tornado hitting the area was high. Therefore, I always knew all of the precautions to take in a storm, and the sirens on Wednesday afternoons were a familiar reminder of where I lived and the potential dangers of a tornado.

I am not sure whether that is why *The Wizard of Oz* was such a popular movie with my siblings and me when we were kids or whether it would have been popular anywhere we lived, but I can remember watching that movie many times and being excited when the Wicked Witch of the West melted.

Several decades later, I learned about the Broadway musical *Wicked*. I knew it had something to do with *The Wizard of Oz*, but I really did not know the storyline. I had heard that the music was wonderful, so when the show came to the Seattle area, I decided that going to it with my husband and two daughters would be a great fiftieth birthday present for me, so my husband bought the tickets and off we went.

I had no idea what would come next! We found our seats and the show started. The story was about two girls who had magical powers and went to school together. Both young girls came from different backgrounds, had different personalities, and liked differ-ent things. The biggest difference, however, was that one young girl had green skin. The other had white skin.

The green-skinned girl, Elphaba, had a lot of compassion for people and wanted to serve others. She had certain talents, but people just could not get past her greenness. When she became a grown woman and tried to connect with other women, it was difficult for her and she was bullied because of her skin color. Finally, it got so bad that people began making up lies about her just because of their own fears or prejudices. People believed her green skin con-noted wickedness.

Elphaba became good friends with Glinda. Eventually, Elphaba knew she would have to leave her town behind and go somewhere she would be accepted for who she really was. She wanted so much for her friend Glinda to come along, but Glinda had to stay. Elphaba had a cape and broom with which she was going to try to defy gravity and fly, and as much as she wanted her friend to come along, she had to go it alone. She built up the courage to take on the task of leaving the town.

As I watched this musical, it felt as if I were watching my story unfold in front of me. How Elphaba felt was how I had felt through-out my life—as if I were green and people did not know the real me because what they saw on the outside was not me on the inside. I felt as if people did not understand me or what I had to offer the world, and as if I were being bullied and gossiped about by the same people who could not see past my "greenness" or uniqueness.

For the first time in my life, while sitting there in the audience, I wanted to defy gravity and fly above my circumstances instead of trying to hide them or pretend they did not affect me. Maybe I did not think I could do it myself. All I know is that during the intermission, I began writing down thoughts and messages that were coming to me as a result of watching this show.

By the end of the show, I was processing the idea that I would be leaving my job to begin preparation for my new career as a professional speaker. This plan was not what I thought I would be processing at my birthday party!

We all drove to a restaurant after the show. My girls and husband could not figure out what was wrong with me. I just could not seem to get out of my head the idea that I was supposed to quit my job and become a speaker. What did this all mean? Was this a message from God that I was supposed to act on?

It was very hard to concentrate on having fun with my friends and family at dinner when I believed I was going to have to quit my job. The message just seemed so strong. No, it could not really be true; I mean…I needed that money…we needed that income to stay afloat with our bills and other expenses.

I spoke to my husband about it over the next several days and also prayed about it and sought counsel from the Bible. It became clear I was supposed to quit my job, but when? I told my boss about my decision after a week of praying about it. I let him know I needed to leave my job to pursue a speaking career. When he asked me how I knew I needed to leave, I told him God told me. We had such a wonderful, open, and honest conversation about the spiritual things in both of our lives. When I told my coworkers that I was giving notice, it was wonderful to be able to say, "The Lord has asked me to do this, and even though it does not make much sense, I am doing it."

Then the most wonderful thing happened! People began to open up in ways that seemed so real and vulnerable. They shared with me about their hurts, their worries, and their dreams. It was as if mentioning that the Lord was guiding my decision had offered us all a new opportunity to get to know each other on a deeper, more meaningful level.

My last day on the job, I began the quest to become a speaker. I was not sure where to start or what to do, but I just tried to go where I was led and speak with people who showed up in my path. This gave me hope and opened my mind to the possibilities of what my future would be like.

Very soon after I saw *Wicked*, God also told me I was going to write a book. Oh, this was so not what I wanted to do! "Please, Lord, do not make me write *it* down," I pled. I did not like to write, and what I thought the Lord wanted me to speak about was not going to be easy. I needed help!

I attended a networking meeting one day shortly after I quit my job. It took great effort to get there and I arrived very late, but I knew I was supposed to be there, for some reason. I introduced myself to a familiar group of people and told them I was no longer working at my previous place of business, and I was now on my own, becoming a speaker and maybe even an author. After the event, I was approached by a woman who mentioned she had a coach who was helping her become a speaker and published author. I followed her lead and called her coach, and in a few days, we met in person. I knew immediately that he could help me and that I was now on my way to learning how to do what the Lord had asked me to do.

The journey over the last year to get to the point of you reading this book has been nothing short of amazing and divinely appointed. I am learning how to make mistakes in order to move forward. I am learning to listen in ways I have not listened before, and I am learning that if people do not like my "greenness," that is okay. I am learning things about myself that I still need to work on, but also that I am a woman of value regardless of my faults. I am learning there is a time for everything and now is my time. It is my time to tell my story, to live in freedom, and to accept responsibility for the things I have done. It is time for me to open up my heart and soul, to let out the dark things, and to let in more light. It is time for me to give back to my community because it has given me so much. My time has come.

Exercise:

As you think about speaking and sharing your message of hope, here are some questions to ponder:

What have you learned from failure?

_____

_____

_____

_____

_____

What have you learned about grief and loss?

_____

_____

_____

_____

What have you learned about lack and scarcity?

_____

_____

_____

_____

What have you learned from physical illness?

_____

_____

_____

_____

What have you learned from having to be patient?

_____

_____

_____

_____

Maybe now is your time, too. What is your new story? What will you do from here on out? What are lessons you have learned so far that have helped you on your journey to freedom and wholeness? What is God prodding you to consider and investigate? How will you share your message of hope? You will never know until you get started. Life is short and you are the only one who can embrace God's plan for you.

THE POWER OF YOUR WORDS

"Death and life are in the power of the tongue:
and they that love it shall eat the fruit thereof."

— Proverbs 18:21

The old adage "sticks and stones may break my bones but words will never hurt me" is a lie. The words you speak not only to yourself but also to others have the power to hurt, destroy, tear-down, and oppress, and they have the power to heal, create, lift-up, and empower. The words you choose also dictate your thinking, so what does the dialogue in your head sound like? Does your inner voice use kind and pleasant words or unkind and destructive words? How do you communicate with the people around you? How do you allow others to communicate with you? Start listening to what you are putting out to the world and to those you love. Look around your circle of influence and begin to *really* listen. You can choose to use negative words and support negativity, or you can choose to use positive words and perpetuate positivity. The choice is *always* yours. Believe that you are capable, competent, and wonderful because you are! Confirm and affirm through your words that you are these things, and lift yourself and others up through the use of positive and optimistic words!

PEOPLE ARE RESILIENT

Why are some of us so resilient and able to overcome even severe adversity while others crumble and seem so fragile? Many studies, including the ACE (Adverse Childhood Experiences) study, have identified that when children are traumatized, they do not grow certain pathways in the brain. These pathways control cognitive, mental, and social behavior. Certain variables of trauma—for example, child physical abuse and neglect, child sexual abuse, and child emotional abuse—have been determined to increase the likelihood that a child will lack resiliency. This is why some people love God with all their hearts, yet continue to suffer from mental illnesses and debilitating behaviors, such as addictions and compulsive behaviors, that do not serve them.

These studies also indicate that resilience-building systems that include community, culture, spiritual support, attachment and belonging opportunities, and the development of capabilities create hope and can rebuild a person's ability and skill to be resilient!

Somatic illness is another way our bodies act out when we are not able or willing to cope with stress or painful emotions. Somatic illness occurs when your stress levels increase and begin to affect your health. For instance, high stress levels and anxiety have been known to create ulcers, gastrointestinal conditions, headaches, migraines, and even heart conditions and strokes. What is your body trying to tell you? Are you taking good care of yourself? Are you eating healthy foods, getting enough rest, and doing at least moderate exercise on a consistent basis?

When you are taking care of yourself and putting your self-care first, you will naturally be more resilient and better able to handle stress, difficult situations, and the many curve balls of life that come your way unexpectedly. In contrast, when you are rundown, not eating right, and not getting enough rest, you experience stress or anxiety, you are naturally less resilient, and you are less able to cope effectively with your feelings, your responses to difficult situations, and life in general.

Did you know that caffeine, nicotine, and sugar are all stimulants that create stress in your body? Do your best to limit your intake of stimulants and you may notice very quickly how much calmer and better you begin to feel.

What about alcohol and other drugs? Depending on alcohol or other drugs to cope with stress is a sure way to exacerbate your stress. While an occasional drink may create a momentary release and feeling of wellbeing, regular use of alcohol or other drugs to relieve stress can be a double-edged sword. On one edge of the sword, they may work to alleviate the stress temporarily, but on the other edge of the sword, they can be habit-forming and debilitating.

Plenty of other addictions, aside from alcohol and drugs, can distract us from our lives and create crippling consequences, physically, emotionally, and spiritually. Other addictions, such as sex (including pornography), eating disorders, and compulsive spending can be equally devastating. When any of these or other behaviors begin to affect our lives in a negative way, it is a red flag that we need to make a serious change in our life.

As an adult, I was able to ask my childhood abuser why he abused me. He said he thought it was because he had access to pornography at an early age. I did not ask details about how much, how long, or where the pornography came from; however, what I do know is that at a very young age, pornography seemed to be a factor in his curiosity about sex. I want to be very clear that I am not suggesting that if our youth access pornography, it will lead to sexual abuse of others or sexual acts. What I am saying is that it certainly plays a role in how we think about sex and our bodies.

In the past when I have shared with others that I was abused, some people have asked me whether there was a reason why my abuser molested me. Whether there were other reasons involved or other factors leading to the abuse, I am not sure, but one thing he mentioned was pornography. Since this conversation happened over twenty years after the abuse, other things may have been going on for him at the time he abused me that were not mentioned, but pornography was definitely mentioned.

Recently, I listened to two testimonies, one from a young man and one from a young woman, who both talked about how they became addicted to pornography around age ten or eleven after being exposed to it while on the Internet. These young children did not seek out this addiction to pornography at the time.

Instead, it was as if it sought them out! In their stories, they both tell about being on their computers when something popped up on their screens. Curiosity pushed each one to click on the pop up, and sure enough, it led them down a road to pornography. Of course, at the time, these young ones did not understand what they were looking at, but what happened to both of these young children was that for the next ten years they were addicted to pornography. Only later, at age twenty or twenty-one and in recovery were they able to talk about what happened as they shared their testimonials.

These two young adults had the courage to tell the truth about what was binding them up for ten years. One had grown up in a Christian home and one had not. They were very different people, yet this addiction caught both of them. The good news is they both broke free of it. Being able to tell their stories not only brought light to their own secrets, but it also helped many other people come to terms with their own pornography addictions.

Pornography is part of many young people's lives. I didn't grow up in the age of computers, so pornographic images did not "pop-up" without solicitation in front of my eyes on a computer screen, but this situation is happening to the eyes of the world's children. If you are paying attention to your children's history on their computers, which I strongly suggest you do, fantastic! There are many filters and ways to block pornography "pop-ups," but it will be important to stay vigilant about it because we need to know what our children can access.

When I was sharing these young people's testimonials with a close friend, she was very surprised that such young children would be involved in pornography and that they had become addicted. Three days later, I received a call from this same friend who coincidentally has an eleven-year-old child. She told me on the phone she did not want to believe her son would be connected in any way to pornography, but because she was convinced these two people I had shared about had a real story of pornography at age ten, she believed it could happen.

She shared that she reluctantly decided to check her son's computer history, and while she found no pornography on his computer, (they had computer protection), she was stunned to find that he had pornography in his phone history. She and her husband had a very frank and open conversation with their son, and she believes, even though it was probably embarrassing, her son was so glad to have been "caught." Now he is safe from pornography on that device. My friend wanted to tell her other friends about what had happened and what she found, but she struggled with the thought of other people knowing her son was involved with pornography.

I do not know what she chose to do, but I want everyone to know this same thing could be happening to your child, your family member, your students if you are a teacher, your spouse, your friend, or your friend's child. Anyone is susceptible, and no one is exempt. We must not turn a blind eye to what can potentially hook our children's attention and hold them in bondage.

My friend wanted to let me know what she had found because she was grateful that my story had saved her son from "who knows what?" She and her husband were able to take action and keep their child safe as a result. My friend, her husband, and their son are all so brave!

I had another friend who told me she had been a prostitute. She was sexually abused as a child and had many misconceptions about pornography, sex, and love. She believed her body was to be used by men for their pleasure and for her gain. At first, she did not make very much money per business exchange, but she said when she finally received $500 for one time with a man, she knew it meant she was valuable.

She is now out of that business and has a relationship with Jesus. She talks about how she used to think $500 for her services made her feel so valuable. Now she sees herself as priceless in God's eyes. She realized that a prostitute was not what God made her to be, and she is learning how to untangle the lies she has believed about herself, God, her value, love, and so much more. Hope enters when we open up our lives, tell our stories, and begin to allow the truth to set us free!

Exercise:

What behaviors are you practicing that have affected the way you feel about yourself or that have kept you in bondage?

_____

_____

_____

_____

_____

Do you have any addictions you know you need to get some help to conquer? If so, what are they?

_____

_____

_____

_____

To whom can you talk about these issues so you do not have to walk through them alone?

_____

_____

_____

_____

When and where can you get help for these issues? What is your plan and how will you follow through with it?

_____

_____

_____

_____

SUMMARY

Because we all have leadership skills to some degree, we are examples to those around us at home, at work, and in the world. Leaders who are hope-filled have opportunities every day to lead others through adversity while lighting the path. Identify and see the light in others and be the light for others too.

You have something to share and your life experiences are valuable. Do not hide your light from others, but rather, let it shine brightly for all to see! The opportunities you have in this lifetime are limited only by your beliefs about your limitations. It is time to shine! Listen to your inner speech and be mindful about what is coming out of your mouth. You create your life with the power of your words, both negatively and positively.

Your own experiences with overcoming adversity have made you resilient, and you are stronger than you know. Do not get caught up in any behaviors that keep you in bondage, and be watchful of the young people in your lives. Do what you can to protect them from addictions, including pornography. If you are struggling with compulsive behaviors or addiction yourself, seek help now and talk to someone you can trust.

When you are whole in body, mind, and spirit, you become a magnet for others. You become a natural leader, a hope-filled leader, and others become drawn to you and your light. Do your best to be the best example of yourself that you can be and remember it is an inside job. Let it begin with you!

When you need help, reach out for it, and embrace it when it comes. Reach out to others and reach out to God, who will renew your mind and fill your heart with hope. He will fill the hole in your soul. Recognize that your past has made you who you are and know that God will use your past for good. You are resilient and God loves you. He wants to be in a relationship with you.

Remember also that you are always either leading or following. Make sure you are mindful about what you are doing and saying. You may be the best role model someone has, and you have the power within you to lift someone up or tear someone down.

A TREASURE AND A PEARL

You are leading and following in your life all the time, and you are resilient. Your words have power, and you are so much more than your past. When you need help and it comes to you, *embrace* it. You can turn to God and the relationship you have with Him and it will renew your mind and fill you with hope. It turned out that the help I was seeking was to fill the void I had in my life spiritually. In this season of my life, I am so thankful I am able to embrace my past as something God will use for good. I want people all over the world to know how much they are loved by a mighty God and how much He wants to be in a relationship with everyone.

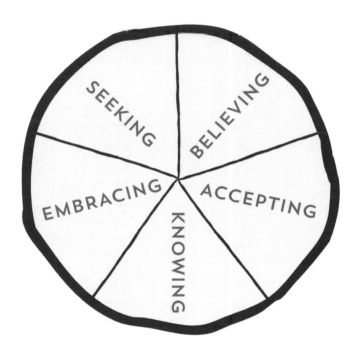

When all the slices are eaten, you will have an empty pie dish, but you will be filled with HOPE!

Chapter Six

HOPE PIE

"He who has hope, has everything."

— Arabian Proverb

In this book, you have learned many valuable lessons, including how to communicate hope in all areas of your life, how to create and find hope in your relationships, both personally and professionally, how hope can help you heal, and as importantly, how your expression of hope can heal others. You have also discovered that all adversity, no matter how devastating, is an opportunity for personal growth and development. Lastly, you have learned that through the use of hope and overcoming adversity, you can gain and practice valuable leadership skills that put you in the position to inspire and give hope to all who cross your path.

PUTTING IT ALL TOGETHER

By reading this book and completing the exercises in each chapter, you have experienced all five pieces of the concept of Hope Pie, and in each preceding chapter, we have discussed the individual slices of Hope Pie:

- Chapter 1 *Seeking:* To attempt to locate, discover, or search for; to endeavor to obtain or reach; to move toward.

- Chapter 2 *Believing:* To accept something as true; feel sure of the truth.

- Chapter 3 *Accepting:* To receive as valid or correct.

- Chapter 4 *Knowing:* To possess knowledge, information, or understanding.

- Chapter 5 *Embracing:* To support (a belief, theory, or change) willingly and enthusiastically.

In this final chapter, you will learn about the concepts of Hope Pie at a deeper level and you will see how all of the pieces of the pie fit together to create the climate and opportunity necessary to express and practice hope in *any* situation. I want to share with you the first part of a transformative poem I wrote *prior* to my healing.

The first half of this poem was written when I accepted Christ as my Savior and forgave the person who sexually abused me. Later, at the end of the chapter, I will share the second half of the poem, which was written a few years later, after I had grown with the Lord in my life. This poem echoes the metamorphosis that occurred inside of me through my journey with God and my use of the pieces of Hope Pie in my own life. The poem is called "Acceptance/ Assurance." Here is the first part of the poem, Acceptance:

ACCEPTANCE

God
I Believe, I think.
I mean:
What a great, powerful,
Loving, caring, forgiving God
He is.
I think.
But
Would this great, loving, God
Put me through hell?
The Pain. The Sorrow.
The Trials. The Confusion.
The Anger.
I struggle with belief.
I guess I have been angry with God
All of these years.
Now
Through my decision to make the
Journey through recovery,
I also decided to find out
About God.
I searched for many months
And
When God knew I was truly ready,
He did help me find
Friends, a Church,
Other Believers, and most of all
Him.

Joy, Excitement for Life, Peace.

These are the feelings I have now.

God does work in mysterious ways.

I'm just glad I'm getting to know Him.

The next thing I'm going to do is

FORGIVE.

I finally figured out how

Through Him.

When I began my personal journey of recovery, I knew I must accept what had happened to me, all of it, in order to be free from it. Acceptance has been painful but cathartic, and it has only been through the grace of God that I have been able to forgive those who have harmed me emotionally, sexually, verbally, and spiritually. Through my unintentional use of Hope Pie, I have also found forgiveness, which has been the biggest gift of all! Now, I want to share Hope Pie with you!

HOPE PIE

Hope Pie is a process, a roadmap, if you will. It models and describes a way to put in language the intangible concept of hope. Through the five combined pieces of the pie, you have a process and a way to understand internally that you do, indeed, have hope. Hope Pie is about identifying a problem and finding a solution. If you are hoping for something, it is because you have a problem, an unfilled need of some kind. You can practice the principles of Hope Pie from a faith perspective or from any other perspective you would like.

Let us go through each piece of the pie. I will use two examples to take you through the process of all five pieces that make up Hope Pie. Example A (Dress Barn) describes what I experienced in my own life when I was losing weight and needed to find some new clothing. Because I do not like shopping at all, I needed to go somewhere to purchase clothes where I could find exceptional customer service. Example B (King County Public Hospital District #4) describes the process of Hope Pie from an organizational perspective. It shows how a business instills hope in individuals and the community through its service delivery.

Slice One of Hope Pie: Seeking

Example A: Dress Barn

When you have a problem and you need a solution, you begin to *seek* answers. You start asking questions, usually of those you know and trust: family, friends, coworkers, or even your trusty computer and the Internet. You begin researching, observing, and compiling data in an effort to make an informed decision. As the process progresses, a few specific answers rise to the top and you begin to feel confident and comfortable with these options, and ready to proceed.

I needed some new clothes but hated shopping. I began asking friends and family where they shopped and where they thought I might be able to get exceptional customer service. Because I was losing weight and had other body image issues, I wanted someone to help me pick out clothes who would be compassionate and discrete and who could help me find styles I could be comfortable in but that were still fashionable. One store in particular stood out above the rest, and upon researching the Dress Barn, I found that its mission included that its customers leave the store feeling even better than when they arrived. The company also has a set of corporate beliefs and values that support trust, relationship-building, encouragement, and that its job is not done until women feel as beautiful on the outside as they are on the inside!

Example B: King County Public Hospital District #4

Millions of Americans struggle with healthcare coverage and are unable to afford costly care. Regular access to a medical provider not only encourages a healthier lifestyle, but it is critical to the timely identification and treatment of adverse health conditions, reducing the need for costly specialty and emergency care, which are the biggest burdens on our current healthcare system. At a time when our nation faces challenges with healthcare coverage, the local hospital and its clinics in Snoqualmie, Washington decided it was time to begin *seeking* an innovative solution to meet the healthcare needs of its rural community.

Seeking includes doing the necessary research (which may include phone calls, reading information, or searching the Internet) to begin finding and brainstorming potential solutions and rule out choices that are not feasible. When we have chosen some viable potential options, we are then at the next slice of pie: *Believing*.

Slice Two of Hope Pie: Believing

Example A: Dress Barn

Because I completed considerable research, made a few phone calls, and had a possible solution to my problem, I began to ask other important questions about my choice such as:

- Is my option affordable?
- Is it accessible to me?
- Is it convenient?

I began to make additional phone calls to find out whether my solution was viable, while asking myself deeper questions that I did not even know I had when I was still seeking. I started forming a belief system around my choice to go to Dress Barn and began *believing* I had found my best possible solution.

Example B: King County Public Hospital District #4

The King County Public Hospital District did considerable research and decided to develop a program called "Affordable Access," which would help those who needed it most by providing affordable and comprehensive medical services. Because of this availability of services to people who would have otherwise gone without, the people served began *believing* they finally had a solution to their health problems.

According to the hospital's Vice President of Medical Affairs, "All too often we see people in our community who delay seeking healthcare when they need it, because of cost. We took this on as a problem, which we wanted to address. We wanted to develop an option for people that would allow them access to primary care when they needed it and that would be affordable." Another medical provider says, "The response from patients has been overwhelmingly enthusiastic. Many of them are relieved to hear about an option that meets their needs." While the Affordable Access program does not cover specialist or emergency care, just clearing the financial barriers to seeing a primary care provider can produce dramatic results.

One client of the hospital said she feels she is living proof of the importance of affordable medical care. She found herself unemployed and uninsured after the company she worked for went out of business. The staff at her clinic urged her to try the Affordable Access program. After years of caring for family members, she was finally able to get care for herself.

Once the *belief* in a solution has been established, we are led to slice three of the pie: *Accepting*.

Slice Three of Hope Pie: Accepting

Example A: Dress Barn

Because I chose Dress Barn as the most appropriate solution to my problem, it was time to take the next step by making an appointment and committing to this solution through action. While I still may have had other options, I chose to move forward in an effort to solve my problem with the full understanding that I could always return to my list of possible solutions, pick the next potential solution, and move toward it should the Dress Barn option not work out well for me. I had *accepted* Dress Barn as the best solution for me.

Example B: King County Public Hospital District #4

One patient, who is self-employed, stated that her catastrophic insurance plan had no coverage for medical office visits. "I'm never sick!" she exclaimed, explaining why that type of insurance seemed to meet her needs at the time. When the Affordable Access program became available in August 2009, she signed up to round out her coverage, just in case. By mid-February, she was not feeling well; she was very tired and thirsty. She went in for a check-up and had some extra lab work done to help evaluate her symptoms. The next day, she was contacted with the results and directed to the hospital for a blood transfusion. She was critically anemic.

"I was on the verge of going into a coma," she said. "I needed four units of blood and spent three days in the hospital." She doubts she would have bothered to go in for an exam if the Affordable Access program had not made it so easy. "I would have waited—I had no acute pain. I could have passed out while driving or going down stairs." Because this member reached out and *accepted* the help of the Affordable Access program, she avoided critical illness and potentially even death.

Accepting a solution brings us to the fourth slice of Hope Pie: *Knowing.*

Slice Four of Hope Pie: Knowing

Example A: Dress Barn

After visiting the Dress Barn and having a fantastic experience, I knew I had found my solution. The clerk was courteous, helpful, patient, and compassionate, and she helped me find exactly what it was I was looking for. I can now go to Dress Barn and get my needs met, I am building a relationship with the staff there, and I have developed a rapport of trust and understanding. I refer others to Dress Barn because of my own positive experience and the knowledge that because it has met my needs, it may be able to assist others with their needs as well. This state of *knowing* firmly plants my feet at slice five of Hope Pie.

Example B: King County Public Hospital District #4

The Affordable Access program is available to everyone, and it allows members unlimited visits for primary care. In addition to being able to self-pay, anyone can give this gift of hope by paying for family and friends to be in this program. Employers may also choose to pay on behalf of their employees to be in the program. Members can choose among six medical providers at the clinic that offer this program. The Affordable Access program provides a cost-effective and convenient way for people to receive primary health-care services. There is a one-time registration fee of $45, a monthly membership fee of $30, and a $5 visit fee each time a member comes to the clinic.

One patient explains, "With access to this program, we don't have to make a decision about taking ourselves or our children to the doctor based on our ability to pay a big bill. When one of our kids is sick, we just call and make an appointment and get them right into the clinic. It provides a lot of security for us."

The King County Public Hospital District's model of doing business provides members with the *knowing* that they will be provided with cost-effective and comprehensive medical care and that they have a safety net for themselves and their families. What a great service!

Knowing you are in good hands and knowing your needs will be met provides the brick and mortar to begin building a firm foundation for hope! Now we can begin *embracing* the solution and begin healing, both inside and out!

Slice Five of Hope Pie: Embracing

Example A: Dress Barn

Now I know the solution (Dress Barn) and I am married to it. I refer others to Dress Barn, I tell others about my positive experiences there, and although I know it may not be everybody's solution, it has worked well for me, and I am willing to shout it from the mountaintop because it has given me hope. This solution, service, and product has met all of my criteria. I have found the hope I originally was seeking, and I am now able to *embrace* and share the solution!

Example B: King County Public Hospital District #4

During a routine exam, one medical provider found a lump in a patient's breast. A mammogram proved it cancerous. "Had I ignored it, I'd probably be dead now," says the patient. "I'm so glad that my medical provider had that program." While still facing further surgery, she is optimistic about her outcome. Her timely diagnosis caught the cancer at a treatable stage. She accepted and *embraced* the help offered by the Affordable Access program, and in fact, it became a lifeline for her and proved to be the best solution.

Can you see how these pieces of the pie fit together now and how the combination of the pieces of the pie completes the circle of hope? This model can be used in all of your life areas. You can use it to find healing in your personal life, to grow your business in your professional life, and most importantly, to build a personal and loving relationship with God. Consider the following questions:

Exercise:

Can you now see the value in the process of Hope Pie and how each individual piece of the pie fits together to create hope? List all five slices.

_____

_____

_____

_____

Could you now imagine what would happen if you used these principles of Hope Pie in all of your life areas? What are some ways your life would change as a result?

_____

_____

_____

_____

How would your family benefit from your teaching and modeling Hope Pie at home?

_____

_____

_____

_____

How could your business or your employer be a benefit to your/its customers if it were committed to using the principles of Hope Pie in the workplace?

_____

_____

_____

_____

How would your relationship with yourself, with God, and with your loved ones change because of you practicing Hope Pie?

_____

_____

_____

_____

SUMMARY

Remember the many principles you have learned about in this book including:

- The truth shall set you free.
- Turn from wrath by practicing love and forgiveness.
- Practice your new tools to cope with loneliness, and don't be afraid to ask for help.
- Understand that you are valuable and worthy no matter what you have been through.
- Seek to understand and forgive others.
- You are not your circumstances, and everything you have been through has made you the amazing and beautiful person you are.
- You are resilient and you are a leader.
- You have a message that will help others and give them hope.
- You are a treasure and a pearl.
- God loves you no matter what.

You can be assured that God is for you, not against you. You can be assured that you have much to give. You can be assured that as you grow, more will be revealed to you and you will find your way, God's way, if you but ask as you trudge the path.

> *"For by grace are ye saved through faith; and that not of yourselves: it is the gift of God: Not of works, lest any man should boast. For we are his workmanship, created in Christ Jesus unto good works, which God hath before ordained that we should walk in them."*
>
> **— Ephesians 2:8-10**

Here is the second part of the poem "Acceptance/Assurance" that I wrote a few years after accepting and receiving Jesus as my Savior. While I only changed it slightly to make it current to that time in my life, the changes in my heart were profound and indescribable, and they still hold true today as I continue to follow the Lord after the past twenty-plus years.

ASSURANCE

God
I Believe, I'm sure.
I mean:
What a great, powerful,
Loving, caring, forgiving God
He is.
I'm sure.
And
I know this great, loving, God will
Put me through trials.
The Pain. The Sorrow.

The Stress. The Trust.
The Growth.
How could I not know?
God has never failed me
All of these years.
Now
Through my decision to continue
To trust Him,
I also decided to find out more
About God.
I searched through many Psalms
And
When God knew I was truly ready,
He did help me learn more about
Friends, my Church,
Other Believers, and most of all
Him.
Joy, Excitement for Life, Peace.
These are the feelings I still have.
God does work in mysterious ways.
I'm glad I'm getting to know Him more.
The one thing I continue to do is
PRAY.
I finally figured out how
Through Him.

So many people in the world suffer from hopelessness. You are now in the unique position not only to receive a new infusion of hope in your own life, but to provide others with hope in their lives. If you know what it is that someone needs from you to gain hope, you can use the process of Hope Pie to help that person to resolve his or her problems. When you are in doubt, you can ask your Creator to help you find the best way to give hope to others. You can be a beacon of hope in all areas of your life: at home with your family and loved ones, at work, and anywhere you stand. You can be the best example anyone has of hope.

Be aware of how you can contribute to the hope of others. Tap into and be aware of God's plan for you. Your life, your very heartbeat, belongs to God, and if you listen to His prodding, if you follow His lead, there is nothing you cannot overcome. This book is tangible evidence that you can overcome anything and share *your* message with the world. Your time has come! Seek, Believe, Accept, Know, and Embrace God's solution for your life, God's hope and assurance for you, and the gifts He has given specifically to you to share with the world.

A TREASURE AND A PEARL

Seeking + Believing + Accepting + Knowing + Embracing = Hope Pie! It all adds up to Hope! All along, I have been talking about how I had a problem that needed solving. I was not sure exactly what the problem was, and for sure, I did not know the solution, but one thing I did know: the help I needed comes from Jesus and Jesus is my Hope.

Secrets can be so damaging and the truth really can set you free! As you become free from your secrets, you will find hope and the light will shine through your pain. That is The Hope Factor!

A FINAL NOTE

"Those things, which ye have both learned, and received, and heard, and seen in me, do: and the God of peace shall be with you."

— **Philippians 4:9**

HAVE OPTIMISM AND PASSION EVERY DAY

Thank you for taking this journey and beginning the lifelong journey of understanding The Hope Factor in your life and in the world all around you. What will you do now that you have learned the concepts of Hope Pie and have received these new ideas and tools? What will you do now that you have heard these stories of victory and have seen hope through a new set of lenses?

If some of the stories in this book resonated with you, maybe you are ready now to take action and use your knowledge. I am happy to share with you that the God of peace is with you. Make the decision about what you will do now. Think about what brings you the most joy and passion in your life and take action.

I challenge you to identify the ten most important action items you have decided to act upon as a result of reading this book and working through the exercises in it. Write them down and keep them available. Review and practice them daily!

1. _____

_____

2. _____

_____

3. _____

_____

4. _____

_____

5. _____

_____

6. _____

_____

7. _____

_____

8. _____

_____

9. _____

_____

10. _____

_____

In this book, you learned about Hope Pie and how each slice of the pie brought you to the final destination of finding Hope, and you learned that hope is woven into the fabric of our lives. We have a choice to seek hope or to give up. We make the choice to live with optimism and to pursue our passion or not.

I would love to connect with you to hear what you have learned about yourself and the progress you have made as a result of this journey. What did you like? What surprised you? What new ideas and revelations have you had? Which parts were difficult to understand or to relate to, and which parts did you not like? What has given you comfort (a newfound peace), and what has soothed your soul? I care about how you feel and I want to hear about what concerns you. Call or text me at (425) 246-9355 or feel free to email me at sue@hopeallowed.com. You can also visit my website at www.HopeAllowed.com or send me a letter at: P.O. Box 165 North Bend, WA 98045

I know I will be as blessed and inspired by you as I hope you have been by me. I would be happy to provide you with a confidential 30-60 minute complimentary consultation to talk more about how I can help you develop The Hope Factor in your life and business.

May God bless you throughout your life!

Your friend,

Sue Mocker

YOU DON'T HAVE
TO BE ABUSED

"The wound is the place where the light enters you."

— **Rumi**

If you are someone who recognizes you are being abused or you realize that in your past you have been abused and would like help, please consider the numbers below as a start.

This book is not all about abuse, but certainly you have read here many stories about how abuse has affected me personally. I know that my past childhood sexual abuse was devastating and drastically affected my thoughts on what love looks like, especially from a man. Therefore, little did I know that since I learned as a child a distorted sense of what love was through my abuse, I gravitated toward that type of love in relationships.

You have read about several things that happened in my former marriage to Max in this book. I may not have come right out and said that certain things he did were abusive, but I want to make clear that you don't have to be physically abused to be in a domestic violence situation—there are many other kinds of abuse including but not limited to verbal, emotional, sexual, and spiritual abuse. I had to come to the realization that the relationship with my former husband was abusive. I didn't want to call it abuse. I gave excuses for why I deserved to be treated a certain way and thought that was love. I learned to turn off the "gut feeling" of when something isn't right. I believed his lies that I was at fault for things, that I wasn't beautiful, that I deserved to be treated in an unkind way, that I deserved something less than others because I was bad. Until I decided that my wounded heart was the very place that I could begin to see that there was light, I couldn't begin to heal. When I saw the light shining through my bedroom window as I asked God what to do to heal my wounded heart, and I saw the shadow of the cross, I knew there would be healing some day, and I knew that I wasn't alone.

You are not alone. There is light! There is hope! You are brave!

If you need help, phone calls to the following numbers are confidential and will give you guidance on what steps you can take to be safe and know that you are not alone. You are a precious son or daughter of God and He loves you so much.

National Domestic Violence Hotline:
1-800-799-SAFE (7233)

The National Domestic Violence Hotline connects individuals to help in their area by using a nationwide database that includes detailed information about domestic violence shelters, other emergency shelters, legal advocacy and assistance programs, and social service programs. Help is available in English or Spanish,

24 hours a day, 7 days a week. Interpreters are available to translate 139 additional languages.

National Sexual Assault Hotline:
1-800-656-HOPE (4673)

This hotline is also referred to as RAINN, which stands for Rape Abuse and Incest National Network

If you call either number, it will be confidential. The operators will have no record of your number, and they will only know who you are if you want them to know.

ABOUT THE AUTHOR

Sue Mocker is an author, a professional speaker, and a hope consultant. She is intimately engaged in the spheres of healthcare, ministry, leadership, education, and businesses involving matters of the heart. Her humorous and touching stories strike a personal chord in unexpected ways, helping peel away the layers that build up over time to reveal who we are on the inside. Sue is affectionately known as "The Hope Lady." Her vulnerability and authenticity help convey her message of Hope in a beautiful and heartfelt way that inspires people to make transformational changes. She has a sincere desire for people to Have Optimism & Passion Every day (H.O.P.E.).

BOOK SUE MOCKER
TO SPEAK AT YOUR NEXT EVENT

When it comes to choosing a professional speaker for your next event, you will find no one more respected or inspirational, no one who will leave your audience or colleagues with such a renewed passion for life as Sue Mocker. She is one of the most gifted speakers of our generation.

Whether your audience is 10 or 10,000, in North America or abroad, Sue Mocker can deliver a customized message of inspiration for your meeting or conference. Sue understands your audience does not want to hear a lecture; rather, people are interested in hearing real stories of inspiration, achievement, and overcoming adversity in life.

As a result, Sue Mocker's speaking philosophy is to humor, entertain, and inspire your audience with passion and a genuine desire to meet the audience members right where they are. If you are looking for a memorable speaker who will leave your audience wanting more, then book Sue Mocker today.

To see a highlight video of Sue Mocker and find out whether she is available for your next event, visit her website below. Then contact her to schedule a complimentary pre-speech interview by phone:

www.HopeAllowed.com
sue@hopeallowed.com
425-246-9355